Spirit Of Love

Spirit Of Love

Ramanlal Morarjee

authorHOUSE®

AuthorHouse™
1663 Liberty Drive
Bloomington, IN 47403
www.authorhouse.com
Phone: 1-800-839-8640

First published by AuthorHouse   11/28/2011

ISBN: 978-1-4567-8690-8 (sc)
ISBN: 978-1-4567-8691-5 (ebk)

Printed in the United States of America

DEDICATION

To my late wife DHANIBEN (aka RAMABEN)

ACKNOWLEDGEMENTS

I am indebted for the general advice received from
SUE JOHNSON, GILL SMITH, Mrs. Thea McIntyre,
Mrs. SEEMA PATEL and Mr. BHANUBHAI MASTER.

Contents

ALONE BY THE RIVER BANK

The boat sailed through the undulating waters of the river. The sun glowed from underneath the water surface covered with the fallen flower petals. Rahul reflected on the happy moments of his life together with Rakhi, his wife. They often walked this way during their younger days.

Their hands held they looked lovingly into each other's eyes. Love was in the spring. Shortly, they would look at the glowing sunlight on the water surface. A passing boat disturbed the water, sending ripples to create the sun dance. He would look at her face and say,

"You are gorgeous, my darling" Her face reflected the pink hue and a gentle smile.

They would stroll down by the bank watching the sailboats making their way through many obstacles. The repair yards for the boats seemed always busy. Life appeared no different from those boats floating by. The gentle breeze, fluttering sails and little flags, reminded him of the happy times. The obstacles reminded him of the sad moments of life. Rakhi often said that he was too philosophical. He took pride in her comments. He would give her kiss and say,

"Thank you my darling"

As the years passed by, she could not manage to sail with him. He tried to assist her, with total loyalty, to improve her life. However, she gave up, being too tired of life, full of disappointments and insulted by people around her. She appreciated his help with a feeling of sorrow for him. When she gave up the will to live, he lost his soul.

The urn full of her ash lay in the garden shed for almost eight months. All that time he wandered everywhere. People advised him to get involved in some activities. Lonely, fragile and indecisive, he couldn't forget her. Food, holidays, people, company, sleeping and walking, music, films and viewing television programmes were not of interest to him.

One day, the boat carried the family members and the urn to the place where they used to walk. It was the same river and the same sunlight reflecting from the surface of the water. As he starred unseeingly at that surface, his eyes became full of tears causing his vision to blur.

After a small ceremony, consisting of the offerings of Holy Ganges water and rice with the leaves of sacred TULSI petals, all of them offered prayers for the eternal life of the soul of his wife.

Now she would never to come back to share his life. He cried. He saw the flotilla of the rose and TULSI petals with the grey ash flowing away on the water. The sun set as he had the last glimpse of the flotilla. There was no sparkle of the setting sun in the water.

As the boat made a slow journey back to the pier, the slow stream of tears from many fell onto the dark floor of the boat.

Now Rahul walked alone by the river bank.

THE MANGO PICKING

Rahul had heard several stories of Rakhi's childhood adventures. During a summer, they often went to Wembley, Middlesex, to buy vegetables, fruits and groceries. Both liked mangos and usually bought two boxes of them. Rakhi liked mango pulp and Rahul liked diced pieces of mango with 'Puri', (fried small round chapatti). Her story about mango picking adventure came to his forehead.

It was lunch time in the village school. It was very hot at midday in the month of May. Young boys and girls from surrounding villages and from Rakhi's village attended primary school located near her house. The children brought lunch boxes containing curry, rice and chapattis.

There was an unmistakable aroma of fresh green mangoes in the air. After lunch, the children played games. Rakhi, aged nine, hastily headed for the mango farm, just on the other side of the school's boundary. She climbed a twenty feet tall mango tree with her feet and hands hugged tightly around the hardened dark brown tree trunk and sat on the first branch where she spotted one nearly ripened mango. She looked around to see if the owner of the farm was looking for a ripe mango, the first sign of harvesting.

She saw her school friends coming towards the tree. One of them spotted her.

"Hey look, there's Rakhi. No wonder we couldn't find her during the lunch break."

"Hey Rakhi, what are you doing up there?"

"Shusssh, if the farmer hears you lot we all will be in trouble. I am here because of this first, golden ripened mango. I want to pick it." She wiped the perspiration off her face.

"Rakhi, be careful, you might fall and then we all will be in trouble. Quick, pluck the mango and come down." said someone in a low voice.

3

Rakhi held the branch with one hand and bent to pluck the dangling mango. She could barely reach it. She tried several times without catching the fruit. She nearly toppled over once. The girls on the ground below were concerned about Rakhi. Then, Rakhi had an idea. She swung the stem of the mango like a pendulum.

"What are you doing, Rakhi? The mango will be damaged if it falls. Be careful."

"I am trying to catch the mango by swinging it to and fro." Just as she was swinging it, she snatched the mango. There were cheers among the girls. Rakhi gently cleaned the fruit and took a deep breath. She brought it to her nose and took a long sniff.

"AAhh! What a fragrance. Just right for eating," she said.

"Hey, you aren't going to eat it by yourself, are you?"

"Why not? I saw it first and caught it by myself. Don't think that I am going to share with you lot." Rakhi appeared very serious as she said that.

"That is not fair. We always shared our secrets. Come down and we will plan where to eat it." One of the girls stated.

All of a sudden, Rakhi saw an old man, with a long stick over his shoulders, walking towards the tree.

"Quick, you lot go and hide. The old man's coming towards us."

They scattered towards nearby piles of chopped wooden planks and hid behind them. The man saw one of them and shouted,

"Hey you, where do you think you are going? Is that Radha? Stop."

Radha stopped. Her school uniform was wet with sweat. Perspiration dribbled down her face. She saw the mirage-like face of the man. His eyes were red and he smelt of alcohol.

"You are the village priest's daughter, aren't you?"

"Yes", she croaked.

"What are you doing here in this midday sun?"

"I came for urination," she uttered shyly.

"Well, couldn't you find a place near the school? Go, get out from here, and never come again by yourself."

Radha ran like an arrow in flight. Rakhi sat quietly on the branch wiping the perspiration from her face. Luckily, the man didn't see her. He walked past the tree and glanced fleetingly towards the upper part of the tree. He was trying to find a ripe mango. As soon as he disappeared, Rakhi's friends came out of the hiding.

"Hey Rakhi, now would you get down before the old man comes back? Can you come down by yourself?"

"Why not? I climbed the tree, didn't I?" She came down half way and then jumped, clutching the mango. The girls gathered round her and demanded to see the mango.

They licked their lips as they admired the fruit.

"Where are we going to eat it?" one of the girls enquired hopefully.

"If you all keep this secret, then we will eat it after the school breaks up for to-day. We will meet in the corner of the playing field and make sure that everyone has left the school. Until then, not a word about this to anyone, understood?"

"Yes, yes. Rakhi, you are fantastic. You always do what you want to." said one girl.

They disappeared towards the school. Rakhi hid the mango in a safe place she knew in the school. When the school shut in the evening, girls gathered in the designated place.

"Do you know how I got hold of this knife from Sukar?" said Rakhi as she waved it in the air. Sukar was the caretaker of the school. Rakhi's favourite uncle was the chairperson of the school. She conned Sukar when he refused to give her the knife.

"Sukar, if you don't give me the knife, I will tell my uncle . . . ."

Sukar gave her the knife. They all had a good laugh. Rakhi carved out every slice with a surgical precision and gave one each to her friends. They were very happy because they tasted the first mango of the season.

RAHUL REMEMBERS
ABOUT RAKHI

He reflected back on Rakhi. She was born in 1938 in a small village in Gujarat State where Patel community members were in the majority. The Muslims lived in a smaller gathering in the village and the working labour class people resided in the outskirts. The latter wouldn't be allowed to step inside both, the Mandeers (Temples) and the Mosques. They could pray from the outside. However, there was a great unification of the daily work life relations among these people. The farm workers remained faithful to the landowners. For generations, a labouring family would work only for the landlord who kept them in regular employment and looked after them well.

There were many rows of low level terraced houses, built of bricks and concrete, separated by two storey high buildings here and there, before another set of terraced houses. Very few houses were painted outside. The surrounding countryside consisted of agricultural plots, belonging to the village landlords. In the monsoon season, the fields reflected velvety green rice foliage swaying gently in the wind as the rain poured. In the nearby river, smaller sail boats made their way to various villages. The wet, damp and sticky air made the rice field workers lethargic.

The village was considered big enough to have a bus stand. The privately owned people carrier companies provided services for the passengers who came from surrounding villages. Rakhi's uncle, whose family lived under the same roof as her family members, was the chair person of the local school.

Rakhi was simple honest girl with her own strong views about life, clothes she wore and food she ate. She was clean and liked all things nice and tidy. She would choose a plain light coloured sari and dainty jewellery.

She liked ironed clothes and did not like anyone using her clothes, towels, pillows, and bed sheets. She was pure vegetarian.

Early in the morning, in a typical agrarian society, she would hear the birds chirping and see peacocks pouncing on birds that bothered them. The majestic peacocks are very protective birds. They keep away from some animals and humans. A chick, reared by a human, was very domesticated. Rakhi would see daily the farmers on their way to the farms, with their tools. She disliked the smell of the smoke of BIDI, a hand rolled cigarette, containing home grown tobacco, smoked by the workers. The tobacco was provided daily, in kind, by her aunt. The regular workers had an early morning breakfast consisting of the basic homemade chapatti and left over curry or mango pickles and onions. Rakhi was generous by nature. She would give more food items to her favourite workers. For that, she was lightly told off by her aunt; if the latter gave a very strict warning, the favoured workers would defend Rakhi. Her aunt would look at the workers and say,

"You have spoiled her too much. You lot don't deserve the amount of food so early in the morning. Wait till I tell him (Rakhi's uncle). Some of you might not work on the farm or here in the house in future."

As she walked away, Rakhi imitated her by saying what she said to the workers. They would all laugh and pick up their tools and say to her,

"Now you my dear had better behave yourself. She can be nasty! By the way, thanks for the extra tobacco."

As they walked away, she would smile and say bye to them. So was her generosity which, in later life, became the cause of much pain to her.

After her early morning bath, Rakhi would put on her school uniform consisting of a white top and a brown skirt. On the weekends, she was asked to wear a sari. When she reached the age of thirteen, she was made aware of the importance of personal hygiene and of wearing of a sari properly. But, her aunt was surprised at the ease with which Rakhi demonstrated the method of wearing the sari. Rakhi preferred a colourful sari to a plain white one. The colourful saris were expensive in those days for the members of the farming community. After setting aside the quantity of produce like mangos, rice, and vegetables for home consumption, the excess produce was handed to the cooperative society which paid the market value. Most of the produce consisted of rice, sugarcane, cotton, vegetables and green grass for cattle and oxen. The workers could only dream of new clothes. They wore used items given by their employers.

With the system of payments in kind, very little money changed hands. In fact, some landowners bartered goods regularly with other people for such items as sugar, molasses, milk, wheat and domestic animals.

Rakhi woke up very early and got ready by herself for school. Her aunt always complained about Rakhi's messy hair whenever she combed it. Rakhi always answered,

"Bhabhu, I can't help it if the hairs get tangled up in my sleep."

Rakhi liked to wear her hair in two plaits, each one tied at the end with a red ribbon bow like the spiral blades of a propeller.

"Always the same answer" Bhabhu would say as she unintentionally pulls the hair during combing. When this caused pain, Rakhi would say,

"I won't have you comb my hair. I will go to Jamni, she is so nice and never pulls my hair like you do."

Jamni worked as the house servant. She was Rakhi's favourite worker apart from a young boy servant whom she would tick off if any information about her went to others in the house. He was her secret messenger of the post addressed to her. There was a time after her marriage, when she received no post from Rahul who went abroad for study. When she told her father about it, he wondered if Rahul was drifting away from his daughter. Then, one morning, the boy messenger came running and handed Rahul's letter to Rakhi. She was overjoyed by the fat envelope; she assumed that Rahul must have written a long letter. True indeed, he had written several pages which she very quickly scanned. As she was smiling, her father thought everything must be right. When Rakhi smiled, she looked very radiant compared to her other four sisters. The latter had dark complexions whereas Rakhi's skin was very fair with a touch of pomegranate hue. Her sisters were married off at earlier ages than Rakhi who was fourteen years old at the time of her wedding. Rakhi was fond of a typical home made roti with curried vegetables and yoghurt with cucumber and fresh green chilli. She preferred playing with her friends to participation in the cooking which was done by her aunt.

The nearest cities to her village were about eight kilometres on either side. Her maternal uncle often took her to see the MELAS (funfairs) in the cities when she was eleven years old. She loved a ride on the big wheel; the so called big wheel was no more than ten meters in height. She spent hours looking at the colourful bangles, slippers and toys. She loved eating candyfloss and would tell her uncle that she was enjoying the 'old woman's hairs'. The hustle and bustle didn't bother her.

Presently, in contrast, at home, Rahul found the deserted lounge very troublesome. There was an utter silence and a slight smell of lilac freshener sprayed earlier. There were TV, hi-fi and video machines. The yellow painted walls had the family members' photos. He looked at Rakhi's photo in silver frame and some yellow flowers she liked in a vase. She wore light green sari and blouse and had posed for Rahul who took her picture. It turned out to be the last photo of her. There was no more hearing of Rakhi saying,

"Why did you come home so late? You know I am not feeling well. I am very hungry. What am I going eat?"

Rakhi's first illness began with pain in her lumber area due to serious injuries she received when she fell from the top of the stairs in the house.

He would go to her and hold her face and say,

"You are gorgeous when you are angry. I am sorry but the court hearing of a case went on and on. I came as soon as I could. You know also the traffic situation nowadays."

"Ok, Ok. Get me some food please" She looked tired and desperate for food.

As he did then, Rahul walked into the kitchen to prepare some food for himself that day. He didn't feel like cooking but had no choice. He pictured her standing near the cooker, saying,

"Don't put too much garlic and green chilli. It will be overpowering".

After cooking some vegetable curry and rice, Rahul returned to the living room and picked up her photo and smiled. He remembered the stories she told about her childhood.

Nearer the time of thinking about her marriage, her father reminded Rakhi's aunt,

"Listen, Rakhi is grown up now. Several proposals have been made for her marriage. Can she cook the basic things?"

"Not really. She being twelve years of age is too young to learn cooking. You know she likes to play with her friends. On occasion when I invite her to do chapattis, she would say to me that 'you are here. Why do I want to make chapattis? I am far too young to get in the kitchen. Now, can I have one hot chapatti? I am so hungry and want to eat now'. Bhabhu sat in silence as her husband turned around saying,

"You better teach her now onwards."

Rakhi's father ran a commercial transport business and had influential relations with the owners of the transports in the villages nearby. He was well known for fixing arranged marriages. He stood tall in the society for his entrepreneurship. People living in the faraway places knew him for his social services. When Rakhi heard about the persistent instructions to Bhabhu regarding her learning about the cooking, she began to suspect that something more was going on behind the scenes. She spoke to her friends about this before returning home. They stood momentarily in silence near a place in the village green.

"Hey, they are going to find a man for you. Why else do they force you to learn cooking? I know that my sister faced the same tactics before her marriage. So my sweet friend, get ready for the wedding drums and for being a perfect wife!" her friend teased her.

"Oh, shut up you rogue. I am not going to get married yet." Rakhi replied hurriedly but at the same time she wondered if that was true. She thought she was young and didn't want to marry. Besides, she wasn't ready to live in a strange house of in-laws and cook for them. A thought of having children frightened her. She knew very little about having children.

On her return home from the school, she said to her aunt that she was very tired and did not wish to learn anything. She went to her bed straight away.

"What's the matter with you?" the aunt queried as she went near her bed and put her hand over her head. Her temperature was normal. Rakhi looked nervously at aunt and asked if they were thinking about getting her married.

"My darling daughter, you are now a grown up woman and we must think well of you and your future. Don't worry about the marriage. It's not going to happen now. However, we have received a very good report about the boy and his family. The boy is studying for matriculation in English medium in Bombay. He is clever but of a little dark complexion. Mind you, that may be because this is the hottest month of the year and we are bound to look darker than normal. We will be going to see a girl for your cousin brother, Manu."

Rakhi consoled herself in the fact that she wasn't going to marry immediately.

RAKHI MEETS RAHUL
AT AGE FOURTEEN.

One early morning a car was making its way to the nearby city of Navsari. It's a city of overcrowded business community. It has a variety of trades which cater for the demands of people living in and in its hinterland area. It is some ten kilometres away from Rakhi's village. The city looked like shimmering giant serpent from the distance. The mirage effects had duly begun. The golden dust behind the car was flying high. It was beginning to get hot. Rakhi, her father, uncle, and aunt Bhabhu were going to see the prospective in-laws of Rakhi's cousin, Manu.

"Where are we going?" Rakhi asked, as she played with her hair curl.

"To see mama (maternal uncle)" her aunt replied with a half smile.

Rakhi liked going to her mama's house. Each year, she spent her summer vacations there. Her mami (wife of mama) spoiled her by giving her the things she demanded. She liked colourful bangles, guava and other fruits of local varieties such as mangos, young green tamarind, and yellow berries.

The car took a right turn on to a dusty road from the main road. The flying dust was filtering through the driver's side window; Rakhi felt uncomfortable and began choking.

"Close your window. The dust is getting into my eyes and throat." she complained to the driver, engaged by the uncle.

"Don't close all of it, driver." said her father.

Rakhi noticed that the car was heading in a different direction from the road that led to mama's village. She couldn't see the familiar houses, the hawkers selling vegetables and bananas. It wasn't as dusty as this road.

"This is not the way to mama's." Rakhi lurched forward to observe ahead through the front windscreen.

"We are going to see your new bhabhi (sister-in-law). Now sit back." Aunt pulled her back. It became a bumpy ride.

"Who?" She enquired still playing with the curl.

"She is going to marry Manu."

"But you said we were going to mama's." Rakhi appeared concerned and sad.

"We will be visiting your mama later." consoled the aunt.

A moment later, her uncle, with serious facial expression, looked back and said,

"Look, my dear, you will be seeing a boy too."

Rakhi had a slight difficulty in breathing deep. Momentarily, the sun's rays fell upon her face suggesting as if a new life was about to begin for her. She was upset.

"I don't want to see a boy. You all lied to me." Rakhi said angrily. She nearly cried.

"There, there, my child," as aunt pulled her nearer and continued,

"You can see this wonderful boy and decide whether you like him or not. He is of a dark complexion but a very educated and good boy. He is from Africa. He is studying in Bombay. Don't say no to him."

The news shocked Rakhi. She felt strangely frightened at the prospect of getting married and having children at her age. She had heard about how some men and mothers-in-law could be cruel; they could force her to work long hours and go without enough food. She had very little experience of housework. She felt helpless. She was only fourteen years of age. She liked climbing up and jumping down from the trees; running and playing games with her school friends. The thought of all that stopping flashed through her mind.

Suddenly, the car came to a halt in front of a house by the city pond. In monsoon season, the pond was filled to the top level with fresh water. The local laundrymen washed the customers' clothes on the bank. Some poor fishermen would spread the fishing nets to catch small fish. However, in the month of May, the water level dropped significantly, revealing the mud at the bottom of the pond and shallow water pockets. The pond then became a perfect breeding ground for the mosquitoes and other insects. It smelled in the heat.

There were people standing outside to greet the guests. As they stepped out of the car, the host welcomed them. The men wore thin white long sleeved cotton shirts and trousers, some white and some

12

light blue. No women were present at the front of the house. Rakhi's father and uncle wore long cotton shirts with pale cream jackets and traditional DHOTIU (long piece of hand woven cotton cloth) folded and wrapped around waists. Their waist lines were covered by the long shirts they wore. All men wore new lather slippers. Bhabhu wore plain white sari and blouse. Rakhi also wore white sari and embroidered white blouse.

After the welcoming introductions, the hosting party directed the guests towards the front door of the house. Inside, all the men took their respective seats, the eldest persons sitting in front row of the middle half of the room and the rest sitting around the elders, in the front room. The women went to join the house women in the back room.

Rakhi was nervous. Her feet trembled. She sat beside her aunt. After formal introductions, a woman served refreshments consisting of light spicy snacks, cold lime sorbet and tea. All, except Rakhi, appeared happy and enjoyed the refreshments provided. Rakhi, shaken and nervous by the thought of marriage, drank water. She began to perspire. She kept wiping her forehead with a small handkerchief. There were no fans to cool the rising temperature. She ignored the greetings from some ladies; her bewildered eyes began to search for the boy chosen for her.

Meanwhile, a beautiful young girl, Reena seemed to be making her way to the nearby steep staircase.

"That is your bhabhi (Sister-in-law) to be. Like her?" her aunt pointed out.

Rakhi nodded affirmatively and said,

"Why is she going upstairs?"

"To see Manu. Later on, you will be going upstairs to see the boy."

Rakhi felt the fright of climbing those steps, not that she could not, but for the thought of seeing someone strange up there. Her feet were trembling still. She eyed the rope that hung beside the steps. Persons going up or coming down would hold on to it to stop themselves from falling. She kept on glancing at the staircase. After half an hour, Reena hurriedly came down. She was smiling. She almost ran to her mother, Meera who knew at once that Reena was happy about Manu.

Manu came down and informed his family about the meeting Reena. Manu's family members went at the back of the house in the open and enquired about Reena. Manu's father asked,

"Well, what is your view about the girl? Did you like her?"

"Dad, she is OK. She had passed seventh year examination. She can cook a little and do house work. I liked her" said Manu with a smile.

Women began to chat loudly about the event. One of them exclaimed,

"Just look at the way these young people meet by themselves, away on the top floor. Our parents didn't allow us to see husbands to be at first and even after the marriages sometimes. Where is this world going to? Then the system of seeing a boy came about, girls were not allowed to say no to the engagement even if they disliked the boy. She would not be allowed to damage the family's respectability."

"You are dead right, Rani. If our parents or village friends saw us entering someone's house or talking to anyone for a length, we were told off for days. Our elders prohibited us from going out of the house to attend functions and all that" added Savita, the woman sitting next to Rani.

"Of course, in a way our life is made miserable by certain women who do wrong. Like that Chhandni, she shouldn't have slept with Mohan. Fancy her doing that!

She is married and did a bad thing with him" Rani added her voice about the past event of Chhandni who, after having the illegitimate child, had to return to her parents. Her husband disowned her.

The men in the front room heard the news about Manu and Reena. One of them shouted,

"Bring that parcel, some rice, kanku (red coloured powder mixed with water), and sweets."

An elderly person suggested that they should wait for the other news of Rahul and Rakhi's meeting.

Rakhi's aunt and a woman brought the items in a circular Thali (plate made of stainless steel) and red, blue and pink coloured saris wrapped beautifully and spread in a fan shape inside a wide circular woven flat basket. Rakhi began to follow her aunt but had to wait near the door leading to the front room. Both women returned to the backroom leaving the goods with the men. Rakhi tugged behind her aunt.

Now it was Rakhi's turn. Her nervousness would not let her aunt's hand go.

"Now go my dear. It will be all right. Mind how you climb those steps." Her aunt instructed sympathetically. Her look assured Rakhi to proceed.

Rakhi took the bold step to face the future. She thought that she was entering a dream world where she would be well cared by the boy she was to like and marry. She became shy as she thought again of having children of her own. Soon she was near the first step of the staircase. Her trembling hand reached for the rope as she took the first step. By the time she tried to climb the second step, she soon came down to the first step. She dwelled back into thinking what if he was not a good person? She would be down in the dumps. Her life would fall to the lowest level in the society. She quickly glanced at her aunt who gestured her to proceed upwards. She realised that if her aunt arranged the meeting, she would have looked into the boy's family background and his character. Rakhi looked at the top of the stairs to see if he was there. She found no one. One more step upward and she looked again at the top. No one was there. After another quick glance at her aunt, Rakhi made the determined effort to go all the way upwards until she made it to the top. There, straight ahead, sat the boy who was to be her life partner. She looked down bashfully. She stood still in front of the boy, Rahul. She began to perspire. She noticed that Rahul sat on a sack full of something. Rahul didn't offer a place to sit. He said,

"What is your name?"

She began to twiddle her fingers.

"Nervous?" Rahul looked at her fingers.

She was startled; she looked up and said,

"Rakhi." She thought he could have asked her to sit on the nearby chair. Since a man's status is considered high in a family, she wouldn't dare to sit on the chair without being asked.

"My name is Rahul. I just finished a matriculation examination in Bombay. I am here to see you with a view to marry you. What about you?"

There was a faint smile on her lips. She gathered her self-control and answered,

"I am in the same situation as you are" She looked away and added,

"I have passed the final examination at school. Then they brought me here."

Rahul responded with a quick smile,

"So we are in the same boat, yeh? Are you ready to get married? Or, have you no choice like me?" They looked at each other and laughed. Rakhi began to feel easy now that the ice was broken. Rahul looked outside the nearby window overlooking the pond, and said,

"I have several cousins who are like my real brothers and you will have to treat them equally. Will you be able to do that?" asked Rahul.

"Yes, I will."

"Do you like reading stories? I like writing stories. Some of my writings have been published in the school magazines," he said, in a desperate attempt to begin a conversation.

"I like reading but I don't write stories."

As they exchanged ideas, Rakhi began to like Rahul. He was strong and of dark complexion. She felt good hearing his husky voice. She began to think that if she must marry someone now, then, this was the person. She didn't know why she felt that way. This was a unique experience for her. As Rahul remained silent, she asked,

"Can I go now? They must be wondering about us." She showed her nervousness again as she twiddled her fingers.

"Oh, let them wait." he replied cheekily.

They both laughed.

"Might as well go," said Rahul.

She literally ran downstairs and hid her face in her aunt's lap.

They knew that all was well with Rakhi.

Rakhi saw Rahul with the predetermined idea that he was going to be her husband for the rest of her life. There was no question of her saying, 'I didn't like the boy'. The same thing applied to Rahul. That is because the parents made extensive enquiries into the respective family life beforehand. They considered how much land one possessed; what the medical status of the family members was; the personal nature of the members, and the credibility of the family in society. Only when everything was approved, was the engagement arranged.

Dinesh, his father Jogi, Meera, Rahul, and Reena gathered in the backyard. Meera was married to Govind, the eldest son in the Jogi family. Govind died two years before in Africa. Although Rahul liked Rakhi, he wasn't keen to get married because he knew very little of the responsibility of a married life. In fact, he knew very little about women. However, the grandfather, Jogi drew his attention to the fact that he would have to go back to Africa as he held the foreign nationality.

The political relations between India and Portugal, over the territorial rights of the latter in places like GOA, DIV and DAMAN on the Western coast of India, were getting worse. There was a real possibility that Rahul would have to leave India. Rahul was born in Mozambique, the province of Portugal, located to the east of South Africa. There was a press release that the citizens of each country would be told to return to their birth place. Also, Jogi emphasized the poor health of Meera and her concern about Rahul's going away. They feared if Rahul would ever be allowed to return to India. The idea they feared most was that Rahul could associate himself with a woman in a foreign country. After seeing the sad face of his mother, Rahul accepted the reality. He thought that Rakhi would care for his mother. Rahul agreed to the marriage.

Rakhi's family was oblivious of this fact. All they knew was that Rahul was to continue with his studies. Rahul's family members were aware that if the political situation was disclosed and that Rahul had to leave India indefinitely, the marriage would not take place. Manu's father, who had a business in Dar-Es-Salaam, had known about conflict of interest between the Indian and Portuguese authorities. There was no general information made available regarding the next step by the authorities. Jogi's other sons, Girther and Rana, residing in Mozambique, were in a better position to know the latest moves regarding Indian citizens in Mozambique.

They then joined the other people in the front room. Both couples sat together to participate in a small engagement ceremony. The leading women from both sides performed the ceremony by presenting envelopes containing token money, garlands, made of red and white fragrant flowers inset with silver threads and colourful saris to the girls, and, coconuts, the envelopes, and garlands to the boys. All had some sweetmeats, made of saffron flavoured milk and nutmeg, and spiced tea, followed by each guest receiving PAN (made of betel leaf, lime and Katho (catechu) before returning to their homes.

Throughout the ceremony, Rakhi sat there with the thoughts of losing all her friends, the family members, the peacocks and the fields, the school, the mango trees and the farm workers. As her Bhabhu approached her to perform a part of the ceremony, Rakhi began to cry having seen the tears in Bhabhu's eyes. Rahul felt very uncomfortable and sorry to see Rakhi cry. Momentarily, he thought that perhaps Rakhi wasn't happy to get engaged to him. He whispered to her quickly,

"Please don't cry. Everything will be OK".

Bhabhu came to her assistance. She smiled as she wiped her tears first and then of Rakhi. She turned to Rahul and said,

"Look after my jewel. We have given her to you now". Bhabhu turned away with more tears.

A NIGHT TO REMEMBER AND THE WEDDING PROCESSION.

Rakhi's brother's marriage was to take place in the bordering village. It was a small place consisting fifty houses. The majority of Patel landlords lived in terraced houses. There were three small shops selling house hold necessities like fruits, vegetables, flours, spices, fuel for domestic usage and seasonal items. The labourers resided in huts located outside the village border. Since Rahul and Rakhi were engaged, the former was invited specially to attend the marriage. Rahul was accompanied by his best friend, Dev. At 4:30 am, all the people attending the wedding arrived in the village. The early arrival was necessary to perform other pre wedding ceremonies during the day time. Dev had breakfast but Rahul couldn't as he had stomach ache. He had left his medicine at home. Moreover, he hadn't slept for two days due to the stress resulting from the sudden imposition of the responsible married life and his own uncertain future. The stomach ache didn't help either. Rahul and Rakhi met for the first time since the engagement day in Navsari city.

Their hearts fluttered during the meeting. She was nervous but smiling and standing by the haystack in the intense heat of the day with her friend Champa.

"Do you wish to contribute towards the marriage of my best friend, Kanta? It is a traditional thing to do." Rakhi enquired timidly.

"I don't know her. Ask the members of my family, they will decide." Rahul simply followed the customary system whereby his elders would decide on such issue. He had no money for such a gift.

"But do you wish to contribute?"

"No, I don't."

Champa standing behind, remarked,

"He will not give you now. You will get what you want afterwards."

Rakhi was startled by Champa's remark. Rakhi didn't take it to mean money. She understood it to be the remark referring to her personal relationship with Rahul after the marriage. She told her to shut up.

Dev offered five rupees to Rakhi but she refused to accept it. Rahul began to walk away.

"Will I be able to continue my education? Will you teach me?"

"Of course, I will." Rahul left with his companion.

Champa admired Rahul's physique and voice too. However, she thought Rahul was very rude.

"Do you really like this guy?" asked Champa.

"I think he is very clever and gorgeous."

"What do you know about him? Don't jump to conclusions. For all I know, he might have met several girls."

"I will clarify it tonight when we meet him again."

They met again at night in the neighbour's house, adjoining the house where the wedding ceremony was taking place. Earlier, many of Rakhi's friends kept seeing Rahul and teased him.

"Can you stop your friends from coming to see me, please?" complained Rahul. Rakhi made no comments; she smiled and walked away, as her aunt called her.

The ceremony finished at half past midnight. Rahul and Rakhi met once more, accompanied by their respective friends. It was a full moon. The stars were twinkling. Rakhi wore a white sari that reflected the faint blue hue of the moonlight and Kajara (a small garland) tied on to one side of her hair at the back.

"Please sit down. I want to talk to you about a lot of things," requested Rahul. She sat down but as Rahul didn't, she got up again and said,

"Tell me first, why haven't you eaten for four days?" Rakhi asked as she came close to him.

"Because I was not feeling well," replied Rahul.

"You should look after yourself."

Rahul made no comment. Rakhi changed the subject.

"What sort of clothing does your mother like?"

"White" said Rahul. He noticed that she often came very near to him, and when someone passed by, she stepped back in the darkness.

"You will have to work very hard to look after my cousins and sisters. Do you remember we spoke about it during our first meeting? We lead a simple life." Rahul stated.

Rakhi nodded and just listened. She then asked,

"How long will you be staying before you go away?"

"I will be with you for five days"

"If you are fond of someone else then our lives will be ruined later on. Is there another woman in your life?" Rakhi was frightened of the answer he might give. It could jeopardise the whole marriage, she thought.

"Has someone advised you to ask me this?"

"No, no, I just asked, that is all. We don't want to ruin our lives, do we?"

"My family is unique as far as the cultural and social matters go. We believe in strict adherence to them. Of course, I have friends and hope that we both will meet and greet them as friends," informed Rahul. Rakhi took it to mean that Rahul possibly had friendships with female students. She was pleased to hear his response; she left the place.

At night, Rahul thought of Rakhi. She looked shy, simple, beautiful, and very courageous and straight forward. He was amazed; He took a deep breath of satisfaction. He noticed how readily she became sad when he didn't give the money she asked for her friend. As he explained to her before, his family members dealt with social matters. He presumed that she would forgive him. In the morning, after the return from the wedding, Rakhi stopped her brother, Manu from waking Rahul. She herself wanted to wake him up.

"Are you awake?"

Rahul heard her soft voice, but pretended he did not.

"Are you listening? Please wake up. Your breakfast is ready. I have brought your tooth paste and brush for you."

Rahul jumped up from the bed and looked at her. He felt the urge to grab her but she smiled at him and hurriedly made her way towards the kitchen. When Rahul was leaving, Rakhi insisted on giving some money as a gift for his younger sister, Reena. It was a traditional thing to give money to the sister-in-law. He didn't take it, hoping she wouldn't feel bad about it.

Rakhi's family members were very happy that she liked Rahul. Also, they felt thankful that Rahul was a learned handsome person who had shown liking for Rakhi. However, they were sad when they learnt that Rahul was to go abroad for further study after a short stay. They felt uneasy about the possibility of Rahul finding another woman abroad.

They discussed their concern with Rakhi and wanted to be sure that Rakhi was aware of the implications of him going abroad. Rakhi took Champa's advice on this matter. Champa said,

"You like him, don't you?"

"Yes"

"How confident are you about him?"

"Everyone in my family thinks he won't let them down. He will be calling me as soon as he can. He wants to study abroad. Unfortunately, he has to go" said Rakhi looking straight into Champa's eyes.

"If you have confidences then tell them that your inner soul strongly believed and accepted that he was the right man. That you decided to stick to him."

The family members were surprised about her strong conviction considering her age. They reflected on her dislike for the boys at school. They remembered how she made her uncle, then the chairperson of the village school, to take stern action against a boy who played a silly prank. The boy unbuttoned the front of his shorts and flashed his penis in front of the girls. The uncle punished the boy severely. She was not to forget this event for many years to come.

Soon, the elders on both sides began preparations for the marriage. By tradition, from now on Rakhi and Rahul wouldn't be allowed to meet before the marriage. There was a lot to do for the wedding. The village elders gathered to prepare the list of guests; to arrange consultation with the village priest for the ascertainment of the suitable days for various ceremonies, such as the pre wedding PUJAS (prayers) of GANPATI (The elephant head god), the MANDAP MAHURAT (the ceremony to set up a canopy under which the wedding ceremony was to be conducted), the SANTEK VIDHI, (the ceremony prior to giving Rakhi away by her guardian parents in presence of the people from Rakhi's maternal side and the chanting of mantras to clear any obstacle due to the star under which she was born). Also, they would prepare a list of the persons who were to be delegated to order the flowers, to decorate the house frontage, for the women, and, for the general ceremonial matters.

Rakhi's friends gathered every day. They joked about Rahul and her in-laws. In particular, they tried to frighten Rakhi by saying that the mother-in-law was very strict about the house duties. Rakhi had no experience of milking cows; of washing clothes; of cooking food; of cleaning the house and of working on farms. However, she would pay no attention to all the frightful conversations. She was dreaming about Rahul and wondering what he might be doing in his village. She could hear her favourite aunt saying to her friends how happy she was about the forthcoming wedding. She declared her concern also about Rakhi's future. She joked about Rahul's dark complexion by saying that 'a crow had taken the delicious white biscuit'. Someone from the crowd of listeners said that the biscuit would go off in a few days time. The aunt shouted back at the speaker to be quiet. The others laughed hearing this argument. All the preparations were going full steam ahead.

On the wedding day, Rahul came very early in the morning, with his entourage of five hundred people, to Rakhi's village. He was received by the male members of Rakhi's family, friends and relatives. The music blared out from the shining instruments of the band consisting of one large and several small drums, two trumpets, one tambourine, a big horn, a harmonium (Small wind driven keyboard type Indian instrument) and a singer. All proceeded at a slow pace towards the reception place. The procession was lead by the band. Inside the place, the large fans, driven by a noisy generator kept in the backyard, were making deafening noise. However, they provided much needed cool air for the comfort of the guests.

At lunch time, several senior female members from Rakhi's family came to the place with specially prepared food consisting of sweet made of wheat flour in the shape of noodles with the complementary Ghee and sugar, freshly made papadum to Rahul's taste, ready made sweetmeats, whole coconut, dried dates, walnuts, and water for Rahul. The rest of the guests were escorted to a shaded area at the back of the place for lunch. The women sang loudly the traditional songs appropriate to the situation in hand. The ladies from Rahul's side joined in the singing too. Rahul was fed by the mother-in-law, Bhabhu. After Rahul had some food, Bhabhu wiped his mouth with water and dried it with white napkin. Then, Bhabhu gave a gold bracelet to Rahul as the first present. All the women sang as if they were holding rivalry between one another. Ladies from Rahul's side would sing loudly criticising the clothing, the food, the provision of small accommodation area for the ceremony, the insufficient numbers of fans and many other things. The ladies from Rakhi's side would reply also in equal terms. They would sing praising Rakhi, their cloths obtained from the famous shops in the big cities nearby, the delicious sweetmeats, obtained from a faraway place well known in India for its quality items. Of course, all these criticisms were a part of the fun. No one seriously felt bad about them. The air in the room was a mixture of multi fragrant perfumes and sweat. The temperature soared well above the tolerance level. The fans were blowing hot air within the confinement of the packed room. The ceremony lasted for half an hour.

Soon, Rahul fell asleep after the women left the room. At noon time, the village went into a hibernating mode. The rows of the low level terraced houses, some painted with bright colours and others simply whitewashed, reflected brightness on to the houses opposite. Most of the people slept for an hour or two. The members of Rakhi's family were busy preparing things for the wedding ceremony in the evening. Some people were busy washing pots and pans in the dimly lit kitchen, located at the back of the house. It had no windows but two open ended entrances. There was no electricity available to the villages. Normally small lanterns provided the light in the evening but this time they had hired petromax lanterns which provided comparatively bright lights. The kitchen walls were covered with black soot due to the use of dried bushes of cotton and other vegetable plants and the dry cakes made of cow dung mixed with wheat husks, for cooking fires.

Because of the intense heat in the day time, the wedding procession left the place in the late evening. Rahul sat in a cabriole that was lavishly decorated with colourful flowers. He wore the traditional items of clothing, a magnificent cream coloured and embroidered silk suit and cap. The band was playing musical tunes of the latest Indian films. The players had put on their finest red coloured uniforms. The places were lit brightly by the petromax lanterns, carried by the persons hired by the band company. The village people showered petals of roses and jasmine flowers on Rahul, his sister and the girls in the family. The village was alive with the joyous atmosphere. The Muslims and the farm workers of the village joined in the procession heading towards Rakhi's house. Rakhi's father, who was well known figure head of the village council, had invited everyone.

THE NIGHT OF THE WEDDING

Rahul sent a note to Rakhi a week before the wedding night.

'My dear Rakhi,

I would appreciate very much if you could consider wearing a white silk sari and Kajara, (a small garland) tied on to one side of your hair at the back. You wore this Kajara on the night of our early meeting. I found you very attractive that way. I would like to carry that image for the rest of my life. I hope you wouldn't be offended by my request. Yours forever Rahul'

She obliged.

Rakhi didn't believe in make-up although her friends had insisted that she wore a light lipstick and a little bit of talcum powder. In those days, make-up was associated only with film stars. However, tradition required the imprint of colourful designs made of henna on her hands and feet. This was a lengthy process lasting for several hours. Rakhi accepted all that but paid particular attention to Rahul's request. Her aunt and family elders wished she would wear a colourful silk sari. They were surprised when Rakhi insisted on wearing a white silk sari. No one knew about Rahul's request.

"Why are you so keen on a white sari now? Normally, you like colourful clothes. What has changed your mind on this very auspicious day in your life?" asked her aunt.

"Bhabhu, I have decided today to wear a very simple sari. It reflects the simplicity of life that I wish to follow. Let us say it is a symbol of harmony."

Bhabhu was very surprised to hear the philosophical statement coming from Rakhi. Tearful, she held Rakhi's face gently and stared into her eyes for a moment. Then, she said,

"May God give you a husband who will take great care of you, my precious little soul."

"Bhabhu, don't cry, you are going to make me cry. He is a wonderful person; you wait and see. He is kind and loving."

"How do you know that, my dear? You met him only a few times," said her aunt as she wiped her tears.

"Trust me Bhabhu" Rakhi assured her.

The others around them expressed their sympathy and joy.

An elderly man stood at the entrance of the room. After a momentary observation, he said,

"Are we going to sit here and do nothing but talk? Soon the groom will arrive at our door; look at you, you are not ready yet". As he left, most of the women vacated the room. Rakhi's friends ensured that her petticoat was firmly worn. They bathed her in her favourite jasmine perfume. Champa noticed the seriousness on Rakhi's face. She asked if everything was OK.

"You know Champa, I am having funny feelings that I never had before. My heart is fluttering about the lack of knowledge about married life. Oh, my God, how will I face it?"

Champa and her other friends smiled. One of them checked the pleats of Rakhi's sari; it needed a slight adjustment of the bit that came over her right shoulder. The tucked bits around her waist also needed securing. As a friend made the adjustments, Champa said,

"You don't go to school to learn all that. It will be easy with the experience. Make sure you tell your prince to take care of you". The girls' laughter rebounded in the room. Then, someone rushed into the room and yelled,

"Stop laughing and get ready. He is just round the corner. You should see him, girls. Wow, he looks like a king sitting on a throne, except that there is no throne. It is that Abdul's creepy crawly and bouncing open taxi! But, you want to see the bright lights and decoration in and outside the car."

All, except Rakhi, got up and went near the window to admire the procession. The girls started giggling and shouting. Abdul looked up and pointed at the girls, saying,

"Rahul, look up there. Fancy choosing all of them?" Rahul smiled and waved at the girls. He could recognise Champa, the girl who always joined Rakhi. He gestured to indicate where Rakhi was. Champa ran to Rakhi and said,

"Hey, get up and come and see your handsome prince. He is calling you."

Rakhi hesitated at first. Champa dragged her near the window. Rakhi kept her distance from the window and tried to look at Rahul. She was delighted to see him for a split second and then ran back to her chair.

"What are you doing that for?" asked Champa.

"Don't you know that it is a bad luck to see your man before the marriage?" answered Rakhi.

"Yes of course, we forgot that, did we not, girls? That entire time madam here met him in the past, that was OK, wasn't it?" said Champa holding the face of Rakhi. They all smiled and as they finalised the preparation of Rakhi, Champa sat next to Rakhi and seriously began to tell her about the girls' feelings at the time of arranged wedding.

"We girls are rather shy to talk about our feelings relating to the proposed marriage. We feel very emotional about the huge chapter in our lives. A mere nod of the head or saying to Mum, 'yes, I like the boy' is all that is needed to set the chain of events leading up to the wedding into action. That would convey to Mum that 'I accept the proposal'. Our feelings are turbulent. We are brought up knowing that ultimately we are meant to leave our homes and become a part of an entirely new family. We are groomed to be able to cook, take care of our siblings, and help with the household chores, so that we are able to fulfil our duties in our married lives. The day that we receive proposals for marriage, we realise that we are on borrowed time with our own family. We are sad about leaving what has been our home for all these years, all the fond memories, friends and family. We are excited about the impending wedding and festivities, the new life, having a home and family of our own. We worry about all the planning and costs of the wedding, what will happen to our family, and how often we will see them etc. We dream of the love and life that we will share with our husbands. Are you listening, Rakhi?"

Rakhi nodded.

"Of course, on the actual day, most brides are jittery and nervous. Each of the ceremonies leading up to the wedding, inch her closer and closer, to this ultimate step of marriage." Champa didn't say anymore.

The sound of music filled every corner of the house and the surrounding district. Small boys were dancing to the music. The canopy-covered place soon filled up with the guests. The elders welcomed them by presenting a rose flower to each guest. The priests began to chant the holy Mantras.

Bhabhu, accompanied by other family women, welcomed Rahul; she placed a garland around Rahul's neck and escorted him to the seat, positioned opposite the similar seat kept for Rakhi. These seats were adorned with colourful silky spreads and soft cushions.

Suddenly, Rakhi felt the sensation that all the things that were part of her daily life were about to be left behind. She thought of the walls, the furniture, the kitchen, the living room, and all the small items such as mirrors, talcum powder, perfumes and slippers, which she frequently used daily. Champa noticed the seriousness on her face.

"What is it, Rakhi?"

"I feel frightened, leaving everything behind. I am going to walk away from my home forever. The thought of making a new home in a strange place terrifies me." Rakhi began to cry.

"Hey, don't cry. That is part of our life. A daughter is a daughter-in-law in someone's family. One day, that will be your own house. Home is what you make of it. Please, don't cry. Everything will work out well, you wait and see. We all wish you a very happy and prosperous married life. Oh, and have lots of children of your own, too." Her friend tried to cheer her up. She added,

"You are looking your radiant best for your Rahul. You should be ecstatically happy and then at the same time would be sad when you see him. It is a see-saw of emotion. It will be dreamlike when you will see the groom. You will be nervous, scared of the future and then again, excited by the future this man holds in his hands. Everything happens so quickly that before you know it you will walk around the holy fire and be declared married! You will then start crying. Happiness and sadness all rolled into one."

There was a faint smile on Rakhi's face.

Meanwhile, two boys held a colourful cloth curtain in the middle of the two seats to separate Rahul and Rakhi; they sat on either side of the curtain. The priest chanted some more Mantras and began to address both sides' people. Briefly, he kept signalling the bride's people to bring the bride to the Mandap (Canopy) and warned the opposite party to be aware of the eminent presence of the bride.

Bhabhu hurriedly came to say that Rakhi should get ready to go to the front of the house and join Rahul. The Brahmin (the priest) was calling Rakhi to be in the Mandap. Rakhi's legs began to tremble. She said to Champa,

"My legs are trembling. I am nervous. Hold me tight lest I tumble."

"Do not worry. I am with you all the way to the place where your dear one is waiting for you." She tried to assure Rakhi.

The band began to play the tune that announced the appearance of the bride in her glory, escorted by the best friends and Bhabhu. Rakhi gradually began to think that she was entering into a new world. 'What would it be like? Rahul is a very nice person. He will rescue me from difficulties. Yes, he will.' She assured her confused mind. Then, she thought of her late mother. She knew very little about her but she wished very much for her presence because she would have been proud and happy to see her daughter getting married to a nice, educated person.

Then, she came out of the house and proceeded towards the fabulously decorated seat opposite to Rahul's. He was waiting for her arrival. As Champa escorted Rakhi towards her seat, Rakhi looked up at Rahul and smiled before taking her seat behind the curtain. Rahul returned the smile and quietly enquired if all was well with her.

"A bit nervous." she uttered from behind the curtain.

The priest continued chanting the Mantras. Reena, Rahul's sister, then went towards Rakhi's side to put the traditional MANGAL SUTRA (Gold chain threaded with shiny black stones) around Rakhi's neck. This is the symbolic chain that Rakhi would wear for the rest of her life. It was a gift from Rahul. Then, several young ladies from each side stood behind the respective persons getting married. They held in their hands small quantities of rice and flower petals. The Brahmin then held the hands of Rakhi and Rahul from underneath the curtain and bonded the hands together by wrapping a silk cloth. Both Rahul and Rakhi felt strange feelings as their hands met. Rakhi thought that she had given herself to Rahul for life and Rahul thought he was having a charming partner of whom he would take care for the rest of the life. After a prolonged ceremony consisting of putting petals, rice and Kanku (RED paste) over the combined hands and chanting of Mantras, the Brahmin suddenly hit a stainless steel Thali (Plate) to announce the bonding of the couple in the presence and witness of all people. The young ladies behind the respective marrying couple threw the petals and rice towards their opposites. At the sound of the Thali, the band players began to play merry music to announce the bonding.

The ladies on both sides started singing loudly the appropriate wedding songs. As the curtain was removed, Rakhi and Rahul could see each other. Soon the priest invited Rakhi's uncle and Bhabhu to indulge in the ceremony whereby they officially gave away Rakhi to Rahul by putting a few petals and rice and Kanku on their joined hands. Champa and her counterpart opposite helped to remove the excess petals, rice and Kanku from the faces of Rakhi and Rahul. Their chairs were then put together. Rakhi kept her head looking down. She felt very shy sitting next to Rahul for the first time. The Brahmin lit the holy fire that began to burn brightly, sending the flickers all around. Someone commented on the scene,

"The flickering lights falling on them enhanced their look" The silver woven in the spreads on the chairs reflected the colourful lights used to decorate the canopy. The band made additional noise by playing more music. The young boys from the village served cold milkshakes to the guests. The whole scene became electrifying.

The priest handed a small bowl of yoghurt to Rahul. He then instructed Rahul to divide the yoghurt into four sections signifying the four directions. Rahul looked at the yoghurt and then towards Rakhi and smiled. He wondered how one could divide yoghurt. The priest noted the confusion and instructed Rahul to just pretend that it was divisible and act accordingly. Rahul followed the instructions while Rakhi observed the process. Then, he was to select a sector and dip his right hand third finger in it and touch the yoghurt-covered finger to his tongue. Then the priest told Rakhi to do the same thing bearing in mind that she used the same sector that Rahul had used. That caused confusion in her mind, as she had no idea which section Rahul had used! She looked up to Rahul who understood the predicament. He pointed a section in the bowl. It didn't matter to him which section Rakhi used. People around the couple laughed. Someone remarked how daft the tradition was. The priest was not happy about the remark. He invited the person who made the remark to see him, for the explanation of the tradition. This ceremony was to bless the couple with a sweet life.

Rakhi realised how silly she was asking Rahul to point out the sector. Later, after the ceremony was over, she apologised for that. Rahul forgave her and suggested that she shouldn't concern herself about it.

The ceremony finished at two, in the early morning. Many people had left the place. The close relatives remained until the departure of the bride and groom at four o'clock. Rakhi's family members were in tears. Bhabhu advised,

"Rakhi my dear, go and live happily. Don't let our family image be tarnished by wrong doings. May God give you the strength to fulfil your duties. From now, your in-laws are your first family members, then us." Bhabhu put her hands on Rakhi's head and blessed her. Both were crying.

"Let her go" said her father as he wiped his tears. Rakhi's friends stood behind Bhabhu. They said good bye as they wiped tears also. Rahul consoled Rakhi and told the driver of the car to move on. A woman stood near the front wheel of the car and performed a small ceremony. She washed the wheel and sprinkled the red KANKU on the tyre; then, she put a betel leaf, one betel nut, and a flower under the tyre. As the car began to move, the woman poured water over the tyre, wishing them a safe journey.

There was a silence for a while in the car, which sped in the direction of Rahul's village. Suddenly, Rakhi burst into tears. The mother-in-law, Meera pulled her gently towards her and said,

"Don't cry Rakhi. I know your feelings. We, the women, have to go through this when we get married. You will be all right. You will be going back in a couple of days to see your Bhabhu and Bapa (Father). OK, now stop crying."

Rahul felt very uneasy at the thought that every woman had to leave her home and settle in with new people. He looked at Rakhi who now stopped crying. After one hour's drive, when they arrived at home, they were tired. As Rakhi stepped out of the car, Champa, who by tradition had to accompany Rakhi, helped her to move towards the front door of the house. Rahul followed her very closely. Both were still clutching the bouquet of flowers and were tied by a long silk scarf. They both entered the house and went to bow to the two earthen pots filled with dry groceries and flower petals. To establish the residency of the ancestors of Rahul's family, the priest had blessed the pots during the pre wedding ceremony at Rahul's place. By bowing them, the couple asked to be blessed by the late ancestors. By this time, both Rakhi and Rahul were feeling very tired. Meera, Rahul's mother, suggested that Rakhi and Champa should retire to a room upstairs. Rahul had his own room upstairs also.

Meera knew that Rahul was to leave in a week's time. She didn't wish to see Rahul and Rakhi sleep together due to the uncertainty of Rahul's return and the possibility of Rakhi getting pregnant.

THE FINAL DEPARTURE

On the sixth day after the marriage, Rahul took leave of all the people of the village. Normally, the village people started work at 6 o'clock in the morning and were asleep by 11 o'clock. The farmers returned home for lunch and had an afternoon siesta. Rahul was to leave by that time. Everyone gathered by the wall surrounding the forecourt of the house to say farewell to Rahul. It was getting very hot. They waited for Rahul to come out of the house. Rahul was popular amongst the community members. His father, Govind had helped many poor people of the village financially and materially. Govind was a very handsome young man. One day, while he was working on his father Jogi's farm, he was met by a sailor who said that there was a plenty of scope to make money in Mozambique. After deliberation, he suggested his uncle Nathu who was working with him to go to Mozambique. So, they left the farm without informing anyone in their families and went with the sailor in 1916. The family members including Meera, Govind's wife were extremely concerned at the disappearance of Govind and the uncle Nathu. In fact, all the villagers were concerned about their disappearance.

Two months later, Jogy received a letter from Govind.

'Dear father and the members of the family,

Nathu uncle and I apologise to everyone for our sudden disappearance. We sailed by a ship for one month to arrive at this place called Del Goba in Africa. It is the main town of Mozambique, a Portuguese territory. Lot of Portuguese people live here and they appear to be friendly. We are living in a garage belonging to the owner of a big wholesale outlet for vegetables. We get a loan of potatoes, carrots, French beans and onions packed in a sack everyday with a set price in Escudos

31

for all the items. We carry sack over our shoulders and walk from house to house shouting about goods we carried. The house wives would stop us and select vegetables and bargain for price. We compromised and accepted the payments. We have become popular with the customers. However, we soon found that carrying a sack load of goods everyday is painfully tiring and we are now looking for a donkey and a second-hand cart. Three days ago, a local black worker told us that he can get what we wanted. The boss at the wholesale warehouse was pleased with our customs. He approved a bulk supply everyday and agreed to accept payments at a weekend. Bapa (Father), we are doing good business. We hope to get a small shop in future with the increase in income. Please inform Meera that I am well. We have learnt to cook basic food and soup. We don't know how to cook a variety of food but all the spices are available. We still live in the garage provided by the boss. He has given us two single beds with sheets and blankets. We take a blanket bath every day. I will make some arrangements for sending money through the sailor who told us about this place. I will write to you regularly. Please note my address at the back of this letter. Yours faithful son, Govind.'

Jogi was speechless after reading aloud Govind's letter. Neither he nor anyone else had an idea as to where Mozambique was. To them, Bombay was far away place. Jogi couldn't fathom where his brother and son were. Meera's mother-in-law, Mani consoled Meera after seeing tears in her eyes. Meera was illiterate and couldn't write to Govind. Most females in the village were illiterate also.

Six months later, Govind informed that they secured a place in the general market to sell vegetables and other household items. He stated that they were living in rented flat and were negotiating for establishing a small shop in the large front room of the landlord's empty property. After three months, Govind informed that they rented the front room and opened vegetables and fruit shop. The business venture turned out to be profitable. In 1935, Meera joined her husband. Rahul was born in 1937. Later on, Govind's three brothers namely Dinesh, Girthar and Rana arrived from India. Reena was born in 1938. The four brothers bought large farms to grow rice, banana, wheat, maize and vegetables which were exported to South Africa, Dar-es-Salam and Kenya.

Govind attended the farms daily. One day, he felt very thirsty while walking around on a farm. He was diabetic. He drank water from the small canal near the farm. He contracted 'Black Water' disease; this affected his urine tract and liver.

He was hospitalised in the town. He suffered excruciating pain during the treatment. Dinesh was present at this time. He called a well-known consultant from the South Africa. A doctor in the hospital injected water in Govind's vein to force urine to flow out. The consultant considered it dangerous and he administered an injection hoping that Govind would come out of the critical danger. Govind never recovered from it and died at the age of 45.

In Govind's village, under the old system, a Desai family dominated the council chair. There were ten Desai families living in a secluded area of the village. The title 'Desai' was accorded to a person appointed by the king, who ruled the area, to collect taxes on behalf of the king. Such person was delegated to form a village council. Because of the Desai's harsh and discriminatory administrative polices, no-one liked the chairperson. However, they found it difficult to vote him out at an annual general election. Those who wanted the remove the Desai family permanently made several efforts to elect another person. But, their properties were confiscated and received physical hardship by the status seeking henchmen of the chairperson.

A handful of village people of various casts decided to unite under the leadership of Govind to fight for the democratic rights of the people. The chairperson threatened them on the day of election.

"Don't try to remove my position. The consequences will be unbearable for you. My appointment is made by the King via district council members. None of you have any management experience for this responsible post. I know who the trouble makers are behind your wish to remove me from the chair. They, including you, will face a serious consequence. So think very carefully about your action."

Govind who stood in one corner of the meeting place scanned his eyes over the crowd of village people and noticed the fear on their faces. None of them mustered up strength to get up and say something to the chair. They were looking at Govind. He addressed the chairperson,

"Respected Desai Sahib, people of this village have suffered from some of the administrative policies you implemented hitherto. As it is, they are living below subsistence level. They have been beaten up by your henchmen. Women have been raped; their small pieces of land have been taken from them and they have been deprived of some basic privileges such as collecting woods for fire and cow dung and husks for making cakes to burn for cooking. They are entitled to these amenities for their livelihood. Not only the poor have suffered but you have quarrelled also with well off families who would not facilitate things as per your wish. Take my own example. You threatened me for taking side of these poor people. Why? Have you not got the right to consider well being of them? With respect Sahib, you either consider their plight for better things for them or I suggest that let another person be elected as chairperson by general votes. As you know, a ruling of India is an elected party by the people, for the people and from the people. That is democracy. Let these people cast their votes for a chairperson's post."

"Govind, you live mostly in Africa. You have come here for a short stay. Why not enjoy your stay instead of mucking in the village affairs? Majority of these are illiterates. To give them something they can't handle for the good of the village life is to invite a disaster for all. Don't you see that? Your family also has the title of Patel, accorded by the king of yester years to impose delegated authority in the village. However, I have been elected as the chairperson from the very beginning and my administration policies have been accepted satisfactorily by the higher authorities hitherto. How my post is a problem for this village? Why are you trying to stir up things for me?"

"I have given my views. I say let these people have their say in running the affairs affecting the life of all people" Govind looked at the people who sat on the dusty ground. They all cheered showing their agreement with Govind.

The majority finally elected a friendly person as chairman. Desai tried his best to oust the elected person by seeking help from the officers at a higher level in the local government. However, he failed to secure the position.

As the Desai family was removed from chairmanship post in the council, people showed their appreciation to Govind for his help in securing a democratic election. Rahul had kept good relations with the people. He visited them during each May vacation and Divali festival time.

Jogi instructed Rahul to bid farewell to the people waiting outside. Rahul went about saying goodbye with his hands clasped and saying the word 'Namaste', meaning 'I bow to God within you'. Some ladies were emotionally disturbed and were crying. They put their hands on Rahul's head and wished him safe journey. Many didn't know where England was. Some exclaimed to him,

"Son, where will you stay? What will you eat?"

"Don't worry, my friends are there and I will seek their advice"

Rahul assured them that everything would be O.K.

The small temple was located inside the village priest's house. Inside, the small dome shaped establishment had three layers of steps upon which various statues of Gods were placed, for example, statues of Krishna, Rama, Shiva and Vishnu and other deities. Every morning, each figure was cleaned and decorated with red and yellow silk cloth, red Kanku imprint and fresh flowers. Several fragrant josh—sticks would be lit. The priest then prayed by simultaneously ringing a small bell with one hand and rotating a yellow metal coated device with several lights incorporated with the other hand in front of the statues. A large bell hung outside the house would be struck to inform the people of the prayers being conducted by the priest. Normally, he conducted two prayers daily, one in the morning and one in the evening. If required, people also visited the temple at different times of the day, depending on the purpose of their prayers. Anyone travelling abroad or going into a hospital would make a point of offering prayers before leaving the house. The priest didn't have to lead the prayers. During festival days of Divali, Holi, Shivratri and Janmasthmi, the priest led the prayers.

Rahul wore a pair of cream coloured silk trousers and a matching short sleeved shirt when he went inside the temple located opposite his house. He prayed for his safe journey and for the wellbeing of his mother and Rakhi. The grandparents wished farewell to Rahul going for further study. Rakhi stood beside her friend Champa. Rakhi was to accompany Rahul as far as Bombay. Dinesh, Suresh, Devi, Reena and Manu joined them also.

His grandmother asked Rahul to sit on a chair so that she could perform the final good wishes ceremony. A small garland was put round his neck and the symbolic RED TILAK (small imprint) with rice was made on his forehead. She put a whole coconut on top of the betel leaf held on his hands. She then put both her hands on his head and rolled down on both sides of the face and said with tears in her eyes,

"My dear son, may God take care of you in the foreign country you are going to. I wish you all the success in your study. Come back soon, for we have no one here to bring my things from the city. I can't rely on the others. Don't forget to throw this coconut into the river before you reach Bombay. A river is considered holy and its water flows into the sea. The latter will be bringing you good luck in England. Don't worry about Rakhi. We will take good care of her. Make sure that you write regularly to her."

She turned around and sat on a chair while the others took their turns to wish good luck to Rahul. He kept looking at Rakhi. For a moment he felt sad about leaving her. But, he realised that he must take one step at a time.

Rakhi gave a red rose to Rahul and looked into his eyes and managed to whisper,

"Please don't forget to write to me. Take care."

She burst into tears and quickly turned towards Champa.

After the conclusion of ceremony, Rahul stood up and went towards his granddad and bowed down to his feet.

"Go well, my son. Finish your study and come back soon." Jogi turned around and wiped his tears. Then, Rahul did the same thing, starting with his grandmother, aunts and uncles and finally shook hands with the cousins. He turned towards Rakhi and Champa and looked straight into Rakhi's eyes, full of tears. By now shaken, Rahul slowly whispered,

"Take care. I will write to you regularly. Please don't cry. Look after Ba".

He quickly made his way outside the door and bowed to the marble statue of his father. He remembered hearing about how his father, Govind, took a sailing ship to Mozambique in 1916. Whereas Rahul was to reach London in 11 hours, his father took a month to reach the coast of Mozambique. After arriving in a totally strange country, his father and his elder uncle, who accompanied him, settled in a small garage. They carried a sack full of potatoes and bananas on their back and walked the streets to sell these to householders. Rahul looked into his father's eyes and thanked him for being the founding father for the family.

Then, he went to sit in the car. As the driver opened the rear door, Rahul's grandmother, against tradition and to the surprise of all present, directed Rakhi to sit with Rahul in the back seat of the car.

Several village people had remained to say good bye to Rahul. One of them said to his friend,

"He is a very clever boy who makes us feel very proud by being the first one to go to London from our village. May God help him?"

The car drove off towards the road taking them to the railway station in the nearby city, Navsari.

Rakhi kept crying during the car journey. Rahul held her hand and whispered:

"Please don't cry. I will write to you often. You will get tired and ill, if you don't stop crying." She tightened her grip on his hand confirming to stop the crying. Soon they arrived at the ticket office. After Suresh collected tickets for all, they crossed a railway bridge to get to the platform. It was jam packed with people and sales persons. The red turbaned porters had taken their places on the platform. They knew about the stoppage places of all carriages.

The huge black engine, hissing and lumbering, came to a halt at the end of the platform area. The train had many dark red coloured coaches which were full of passengers. Some of them were literally hanging outside the compartments. Those due to board and those inside compartments made a deafening noise. The hot weather made some sweat and the smell of it was intolerable. The vendors selling mangos, chhiku and guava fruits, drinks, spicy snacks, biscuits and jasmine garlands for women added fragrances and noise in the air. The passengers wanted to get inside the compartments. Tempers flared when the porters threw parcels and small bags inside compartments; the passengers swore at them for careless behaviours but no serious consequences followed as the train stopped for two minutes only.

Dinesh wore a starched and ironed cream coloured top coat and white Dhoti. He looked concerned about getting all the family members on train. He said to his son Suresh,

"Go quickly; make sure that Manu and Rahul have got inside the compartment."

He gave little extra money to the porters to ensure that all the baggage and family members got on board the train.

The porters faced hassle from passengers who wanted to pay less than the quoted price for service. There was pandemonium on the platform.

A woman with crying baby in her hand begged help from a porter.

"You have to give me two rupees. Have you got the money?"

"Brother, it is vital for me to get this train as my mother-in-law has died this morning. I am going to attend her funeral. I have one rupee only. Have pity on me. Help me please."

The porter looked at the woman and her child. He picked up her hold-all and walked a little distance quickly to find a place for them in the nearby carriage. He shouted at the passenger inside the compartment,

"This woman needs to go to attend a funeral. Can anyone of you make room for her?"

"Let her in" said a man standing near the door. Soon she got on and turned around to give the rupee to the porter. The whistle blew. The porter shouted,

"Sister, go and send your mother-in-law to heaven. Give the rupee to the priest on my behalf."

People were shouting, swearing, hot tempered and pushing to get on the train. The children were crying. The porters carried trunks and other goods on their heads. They began to negotiate, with a slurry voice,

"Come, come, let there be a room. All want to go," for the room inside the compartments for their clients. Rahul and Manu ended up in the front compartment next to the engine. Rakhi and the others managed to get in the last but one compartment.

After a long whistle, the wheels started their lumbering movements. The clickety click rhythm increased as the train gathered the speed.

Rakhi kept herself away from Dinesh and Suresh. She disliked Dinesh staring at her. As a woman, she knew that a man who stared at women like that has nasty intentions. In a short spell of time she had spent at her in-laws house, she observed Dinesh as being a powerful and cunning person, having the final say in all matters. Once, Mani asked Rakhi to join her in the kitchen. Rakhi sat on the kitchen floor near the fire and prepared spices for an item that Ma was to cook. Rakhi was asked to wash some vegetables, prepared for making curry. When she done that, she was asked to take Ma's position near the fire and cook the curry. Rakhi said,

"Ma, I don't know how to cook vegetable curry."

"That I know my child. I want you to learn how to make it as you will be expected to go to the estate soon after Rahul goes abroad. You will have to prepare meals there for all. Sooner you learn the better it is for you."

Presently, Meera arrives into the kitchen and seeing Rakhi doing the cooking on an open fire, she said,

"Ma, she is a young child. She never ever had house training in Sakri."
Meera looked at Rakhi whose eyes were full of tears and said,

"Get up my child and go to Rahul upstairs." Meera sat to prepare the
curry. Amba Ma said,

"Meera, Dinesh told me that Rakhi was doing nothing in this house
since she came here after the marriage. He said that Rakhi will have to
cook for all on the estate as you will have other important things to handle
there. He asked me to teach her about cooking. Tell me, what else can I
do but to show her how to prepare vegetable curry? You know Dinesh's
temper. He doesn't like us ignoring his wish."

"It's OK Ma. I will handle it when it comes to that situation". Ma left
the kitchen and Meera continued with the cooking.

At lunch time, Rakhi was summoned downstairs by Ma as Jogi and
Dinesh made their way to the kitchen. Dinesh stopped near his mother
and said,

"What was Rakhi doing upstairs? She was supposed to be with you
learning how to cook." Dinesh looked at Rakhi passing by him. He said
to her,

"You should be in the kitchen. What were you doing upstairs? Don't
you want to learn cooking?" Dinesh entered the kitchen and took his
place on a wooden platform. Rakhi stood behind Meera. Dinesh looked
at Rakhi and said,

"Do you know how to serve food to people? Don't just stand there
doing nothing"

"I told her to go upstairs. She is a mere child and there will be a plenty
of time to teach her about cooking and other matters." She looked at
Rakhi and said, "Go my child, go back upstairs"

Rakhi left. Dinesh was fuming with anger. He said,

"That's it. Go spoil the girl. What does it matter to me? You will be
there to undertake all the work on the estate. Don't then complain that
you have health problems resulting from over work." Jogi ate quietly up to
then. He looked at Dinesh and said,

"Do you not see Rakhi as our child? There are two young girls in this
house also. Have you told them to learn to cook from now? They will be
gone to a strange house after their marriages with full expertise in cooking
but right now there is no need for them to learn all."

"I think you should not interfere in this matter, Bapa. They will have
to do as they are told. Everyone seems to have a loose tongue in this

house". Dinesh washed his right hand with water in his Thali (Plate) and walked out of the kitchin.

The heat was unbearable. The fans inside the cabin made loud buzzing noises and children were shouting and crying. Everybody felt uncomfortable because of the hot stinky air blowing within the crammed compartment. When the train stopped at the next station, there was an inrush of more shouting and hustling passengers. Rakhi managed to stand in a corner where the smell of urine from the nearby open toilet was unbearable. Her mind was preoccupied with the thought of her future life without Rahul. She thought,

'What will I do if Rahul does not come back early, or, if he falls in love with someone? Why could I not join him on this trip? Who will help me in his absence?'

From her early childhood days, she had been an independent person. She pursued her desired aims relentlessly at any cost. Her three sisters showered tremendous love upon her because her mother died soon after giving birth to her. It was that fact that made her very protectively independent. She was well looked after by her Bhabhu and uncle. Her uncle always favoured her whenever she had a problem and she made the best use of his consideration.

After the marriage, she envisaged hard work at Rahul's place. Before, she didn't learn about such things as cooking, cleaning the house, washing clothes, bed sheets, and all other domestic tasks. She cried literally, whenever she had to perform those duties in a short period of time. Meera and the grandparents kindly gave all the possible help to her. Meera would sit next to Rakhi and give advice on the method of preparing a meal. The grandparents gave moral support to her by praising her cooking. The grandmother strictly and spontaneously commented on anything that was not perfect. She would show Rakhi how to lift beds, clean utensils, the floors and milk the cows. The wooden beds had cotton belt wrapped round to form the base upon which mattress and bed sheets were spread. Several beds were put upright every morning and put down in the evening to prepare for night use.

On many occasions, Rakhi felt offended by comments or accusations from others. However, Meera covered up her mistakes and rescued her from the low down feelings. She remembered what Rahul had said about Meera; that his mother was a very kind, sentimental, and patient person. She had suffered lots of hardship after the death of Govind.

The train stopped suddenly at another station from where Dinesh's big estate could be reached. Rahul stuck his neck out of the compartment to look for his mother. Rakhi couldn't do so as there were too many people to pass by to reach the door or a window.

"Ba, I am here."

He waved his arm and shouted as soon as he spotted her on the crowded platform. Meera heard the familiar voice. She walked a little towards Rahul's compartment. She was crying. She could hardly utter words. From the distance, she heard Rahul:-

"Ba, look after yourselves. Take good care of Rakhi."

Meera waved her arm to Rahul. He could just see her making her way towards him. He wished that mother and Rakhi could have joined him on this trip to England. But, with Dinesh being in total command of the family and farming, no one could argue against him, not even his wife Devi. He had other ideas for them. Meera was to run the estate in his absence, and, Rakhi was to look after the grandparents.

As the whistle blew, the train laboured to pull out from the station. Rahul had a last look at his mother who wore a white sari. He was devastated by the thought that Meera was going to be alone and helpless. Others in the family paid very little attention to her poor health. She suffered from arthritis and a deteriorating valve condition of her heart. Then, there was to be the added responsibility of taking care of Rakhi. She already had plenty to do; she ensured that the food was ready and the cows were milked on time; clothes were washed and dried; fodder and green grass were available to feed the oxen and cows. Meera had very little time for herself. All these flashed through Rahul's mind.

She was sliding away slowly as the train gathered speed. She soon mingled into the wavy mirage of people. Rahul wiped his tears. For the first time, Rahul felt that he didn't want to leave Rakhi behind. He even wished that he could cancel going abroad. However, due to the political upheaval between India and Portugal over the territories of Goa, Div, and Daman in India, he had no choice but to go to England via Mozambique for further studies. Rahul didn't like the education facility which was in the native Portuguese language in Mozambique. He said that he would rather be in England to continue studies in English. Besides, his roommates in the Public school he attended in Andheri, Bombay, were all in the UK.

Dinesh had purchased a flat in a multi-storey building by the famous Marin Drive area of Bombay. Devi was to oversee the children and their education, and look after the flat generally whilst Dinesh remained free to pursue his own things. There were two bedrooms in the flat. Rakhi and Rahul occupied one and Dinesh and Devi slept in the other. Devi insisted that Manu should sleep on the floor of Rahul and Rakhi's room. It had a marble floor, a wooden bed and a small cupboard. Suresh slept in the living room. Because Rakhi and Rahul were very young, Devi was concerned about them having intercourse and possibly Rakhi getting pregnant; hence, Manu shared the room.

Rakhi cried a lot in Rahul's arms. Manu was snoring loudly, so they had chance to whisper.

"Having come near the door of my life, where are you going now? When will you come back?" Rakhi asked with tearful eyes,

"I suppose after five or six years. Don't worry, I will often write to you. Who knows, you might come to me after few years. There, there, don't cry." He wiped her tears.

He kissed her on the cheek and gently caressed the back of her neck. As Rahul went to kiss her lips, he observed her shyness and felt a slight resistance on her part to move closer. He said,

"Your eyes have understood that I am suitable to be yours, then why resist?"

She looked at her own image in his eyes and said,

"Now that we are caught up in this love storm, I don't have any worries about anything, especially now you being my guide for life. You have stolen my dreams anyway."

As Rahul kissed her lips, a sweet vibration ran down his spine and reverberated. He felt a floating sensation. He whispered,

"I want to know the depth of your sea deep heart."

Rakhi lost her focus and felt as if she was floating in the clouds. Her lips began to tremble.

Then, suddenly she tried to move away from him as she foresaw the consequences of intimate moments—that she was only fourteen; she couldn't risk becoming a mother at that age. Champa had warned her about this,

'Remember that you shouldn't fall in the trap of having an intimate relationship with Rahul on your final night in Bombay. Who would look after you if you became pregnant?'

His grip was tight; she could not move away. As he kissed her on the side of her neck and tried to unbutton her blouse, they heard the sudden snoring noise of Manu. Rakhi blushingly turned her face to one side and said,

"Be careful, Manu might wake up."

He pulled her closer. She dug her face into his chest. For a moment, they felt the delightful warmth of their bodies. Rakhi wore a sari. Rahul didn't like it. He wore pyjamas. Then, Manu snored loudly again. As Rahul looked at him, she managed to free herself. For both, this was the first experience of romance.

The next morning came too soon for everyone. They got ready to go to the airport. Before leaving the flat, most of them had breakfast consisting of toasts, cooked spicy potatoes and flaked rice, tea and milk. Rahul and Rakhi didn't have anything. Devi accompanied Rakhi who kept crying. Rahul was in a separate car with the others. The airport building for the departure and arrival of the passengers was partly incomplete due to lack of finance. Inside the departure section, passengers stood in front of various desks for checking in. After he had checked in, Rahul had last look at everyone as he stood near a migration desk and said goodbye to Rakhi and the others. As he turned his back towards them and walked forward to join other passengers, he remembered how he saw his mother disappearing into the crowds on the railway platform. He quickly looked back towards Rakhi who just managed to lift her arm to wave at him melting away in the crowds of passengers.

THE INTERIM PERIOD . . .

On her return from Bombay, Rakhi, accompanied by Champa, was sent to her parents in Sakri. They arrived at the house just before midday. It was hot and stuffy. Most of the villagers were having their afternoon siesta. The front of the terraced house was painted white. The main front door and two side windows were made of thick brown wood. Inside, the house had two large open rooms, the front was the men's living room and the back was a bedroom for the ladies. The dining table was set up in the far corner of the back room. The door nearby led to the kitchen area. Also, a swing was attached to the ceiling of this room. Behind the swing, there were tall wooden cupboards for storing grains. There were no windows on both sides of the rooms. A large door at the end of the back room led to an open area used for many activities such as cleaning pots and washing and drying clothes and fodder. A bathroom was located behind the kitchen.

The interiors of the house provided cool air on hot days. The walls were painted light blue. The three small bedrooms upstairs had front windows each and basic furniture consisting of wooden beds with hard mattresses, cotton bed sheets and pillows and an additional silk covered thick quilt for winter time. Each room had a cupboard and a small dressing table.

Bhabhu came hurriedly to the front door to welcome Rakhi and Champa. She embraced Rakhi and ran her hand from Rakhi's head to her face and said,

"My dear girl, let me hold you tightly, I have missed you so much. I prayed to God to look after you in the stranger's house." She pulled herself back and looked straight in Rakhi's eyes and said,

"Are you well, my dear?"

"Yes"

"Did anyone say unpleasant things to you?"

"No"

"How was Rahul when he left you?"

"Well"

Champa tried to separate Bhabhu from Rakhi, saying,

"That's enough, Bhabhu. Stop asking all the questions. We haven't entered the house yet. All will be revealed to you once we are inside the house. We are very tired and hungry. So let us go inside."

Bhabhu realized the extent of her unease. She held on to Rakhi's hand as she escorted her to the swing in the back room. Both, Rakhi and Bhabhu sat on the swing and Champa took her place on the nearby bed. The wooden swing, decorated with emerald square tiles and a thin mattress with two oblong pillows on either side, was a common feature in most of the houses. It provided relaxation and gentle cool air in the hot weather. Bhabhu shouted for the house maid who quickly appeared in the room. She expressed her happiness for seeing Rakhi. Bhabhu interfered,

"Come, come now, go and prepare the dishes for three of us, we are all hungry."

The maid went in the kitchen and began the preparations for lunch. Bhima had had his lunch earlier already.

"I have prepared your favourite food, my dear. Did you eat well at your in-law's place? You look a bit thin to me" Bhabhu said anxiously to Rakhi.

"Yes, I ate well but there was a lot of work I had to do."

"Bhabhu, I was there with her all the time. Stop worrying for her. Her mother-in-law seemed very kind and considerate. The grand mother-in-law appeared a bit strict but only to make sure that Rakhi picked the right habits generally. The granddad is kind and gentle. I tell you what he did.

One day, the grandmother-in-law was saying something to Rakhi about the milking of the cows. The granddad retorted to his wife,

"Just forget about lecturing your poor daughter-in-law. She is a dainty little girl and you start telling her to do all sorts of work instead of looking after her"

The grandmother looked at Rakhi fleetingly and said,

"Well, well, you seemed to be his favourite already. All right my daughter; tell me all about your Bhabhu and Bapa."

"My Bhabhu is my best mother. She is very caring and gives me what I want. She knows what sort of food I like. She never gets angry at me. She thinks highly of your grandson. My father has temper but never takes out on me. His reputation is very high amongst the people of many villages. He works very hard on the farms."

"Well, that seems alright. Please remember that you command respect from them and give respect to them also." Bhabhu, had to say to Rakhi. Champa laughed a little looking at the radiant face of Bhabhu.

"Wait till your turn comes for marriage. It's not going to be long for you either, my girl. Don't laugh." Bhabhu snapped at Champa.

Lunch consisted of curries, made of aubergine and potato, and, cabbage and peas. In addition, yogurt curry (KADHI), rice, chapattis, mango pickles and papadums were prepared. After lunch, Rakhi and Champa retired upstairs to a bedroom.

Rakhi stood near the window and felt relaxed looking at the birds flying in the sky. The hot air blew on her face. She quickly turned towards Champa and laid on the bed besides her and said,

"Ah, Champa, it is so peaceful here; no one to tell you to do anything. It seems OK at Rahul's place but you aren't free to do anything of your own." Rakhi turned to look at Champa who appeared to listening intently.

"Hey, what are you thinking?"

Champa brought a little smile on her face and said,

"My mother advised me that once you get married, your freedom of thinking and movement go out of the window. However, you are going to be alright. The family members are straight forward people and your mother-in-law is so nice. I think she will be your favourite friend. As to Rahul, well, you tell me about him. Tell me all about your mischief with him." Champa became curious as she sat on the dressing table stool.

"Rahul is very kind and gentle to me. He never once got angry with me but Ba told me that he was hot tempered and I should be aware of it. He is very clever. He showed me his stories and after reading some, I feared how I will match his standard of thinking. When I mentioned this, Rahul took me in his arm and said that I should remain as I am. He loves me the way I am. You wouldn't imagine that he could be a hot tempered person. It was unbearably painful to part from him on the night before his departure for England." Rakhi suddenly turned and looked down towards the floor with her wet eyes. Champa got up hurriedly and sat on Rakhi's bed; she turned Rakhi's face towards her,

"Shush, my friend, don't cry. He will call you soon. He must be getting near London now. I wonder where he will be staying. Let us pray that soon he will find a place to stay. You know, he is very lucky to go to study in London. It is a very honorable opportunity. He will be an English gentleman when you will meet him. Oh, my friend, what will you do?

How will you converse with him? You will be doing left right left and so on. Why not think of attending English classes?" Champa suggested.

"Shut up, you. I wanted to study further but the grand mother-in-law said that I would be taking an interest in other boys and not in the study. How dare she think of me like that? You know how resolute I am about my things." Rakhi was angry.

"What do you expect from an old lady who never went to school and got married at the age of seven? She is merely reflecting the importance of family's credibility. It can easily be tarnished sometimes by a disgraceful act by a member of the family. It is rare and I would ignore it. You find a way to please your grandfather-in-law who can override his wife's decision." Champa threw light on the traditional views.

"I reminded Rahul about my wish to pursue further education, but he had no time to mention it to his grandfather. Most of the members of the house were scared stiff to talk to Dinesh for some reason. I don't like Dinesh; he keeps staring at me. Rahul couldn't stand his accusations to, shouting at, and ordering to persons in the house. Dinesh, even, has angry arguments with his father. Once he bought another car for the use of Jogidada. He said,

"I hope you like the car. It's almost new. I will find a driver. You have to give him food and money. Now you will not have to travel in rickshaws."

"How much did you pay for it?"

"Over a Lakh(100000) rupees."

"Why did you pay so much money when I have difficulty in meeting the cost of living here? How am I going to provide money and food to a driver? I have very little money. The other day you took 30000 rupees from me. You said that you will return it in a month's time. How are you going to do that?" Jogi said angrily.

"This is the trouble with you. When I consider your conveniences you always disagree with me. I didn't take your money for my personal use. It was for the equipments on the estate. What is 30000 rupees? I will return your money tomorrow." Dinesh shouted at his father.

"And where will you get the 30000rupees from? You haven't returned the money you borrowed from me last month. In future, don't ask me to give you any money" Jogi said; he was very upset and walked away towards the back of the house. Tell me, is there a possibility for me to study English?" Rakhi appeared disappointed.

"I suppose you don't have a chance. What will you do when you will face Rahul?"

Before Rakhi could answer to that, Champa suddenly began to smile and said,

"Tempt him heartily all the time! Say to him 'me no English; only Gujarati.'"

Rakhi nearly got up to hit her. Champa laughed away loudly. Suddenly, Rakhi began to cry. Champa hastily embraced her,

"What is it now?"

"Champa, I miss him terribly." Rakhi cried more and began to say in broken words,

"We felt our young love was blossoming and had thought nothing of pain but happiness. Now look at it. He is drifted away for a long time, leaving me to face the loneliness among the crowd."

"Champa, aren't you going to your house?" shouted Bhabhu from downstairs.

"Don't worry Bhabhu, I told them that I would be late coming home" Champa replied. Bhabhu said nothing further. Champa wiped Rakhi's tears and said,

"Don't cry, my sweet friend. You both are destined for this event. Just think, how lonely he will be? At least you have me and others here you could talk to. Poor him; what about his dilemma?"

Rakhi stopped crying slowly.

After a few weeks, Rakhi had to return to her in-laws. She preferred to stay with Ba than to face Dinesh's staring eyes. The latter mostly spent time on the estate. Since Ba was to look after the farm business when Dinesh was out and about, Rakhi had no choice but to spend time with Ba. Rakhi wanted to stay in Pinsad with the grandparents-in-law also as they were no problem to her. The grandfather-in-law, Jogi undertook the responsibility for Rakhi's welfare while Rahul was abroad.

The cousins, aged between seven and fifteen years, were studying in the school near the estate farm. On Rakhi's arrival at the farm, she instantly added love, culture and togetherness into the family. She had all the qualities that a respected family would look for, as she was raised and groomed to be one, by a very noble family in her village. After the marriage, she immediately became the centre and focal point of all the children in the family as she had a heart full of love for children. Whenever she had a bit of free time, she played games with them. They chased her and she hid from them. When she was found, the children would hold her from all direction and laugh a lot saying, 'We found you, we found you'. She offered them small sweets as a reward. The children looked for her to favour them at night to prepare meals and tuck them into bed.

During the HOLI (spring) festival, Rakhi was the most sought after person among all the children as she could be showered with all the colours and bring a smile on the children's faces at the cost of her tears of sheer joy. Hundreds of years ago, a king named KASHYAPPA considered himself as GOD. However, his son, PRAHALLAD didn't agree with his father. The latter tried to kill him in various ways but each time the son survived. The king forced his sister HOLIKA to take the son in her lap and sit on the fire hoping he would get rid of son that way. Holika was burned to death but the son stayed alive. In Gujarat State of India, the festival of HOLI lasts for five days. On day one, a large pile of dried wood and round cakes, made from a mixture of husks and cow dung is burned. Men, women and children throw fresh coconuts and popcorns in the fire. At the end of the burn, youngsters retrieve a piping hot coconut from the ash and roll it for a distance in the cool dust; the boys run a race to capture the coconut. On the second day, village folk pour water on the still smoldering fire. They sing and dance to celebrate the occasion while spraying coloured water and dried powder of various colours on each other. Some went to extremes by adding used diesel oil with water. On the rest of three days, they continue singing and dancing and spraying water and powder.

On one afternoon, when the children were writing letters to Rahul about their examination results, Ba and Devi were resting on their beds. When Rakhi was at her parent's house, Ba had a mild stroke which disabled her right arm. As soon as someone mentioned Rahul's name, Devi would start crying because she missed him. Ba wanted Rakhi to stay with her at the farmhouse. But, Jogi who came to see Ba insisted that Rakhi should be with him in Pinsad. Ba couldn't go against the wish of Jogi who was the head of the family. However, she said,

"God had taken my Ram (Govind) and left me to suffer this life with my children and one and only one my daughter-in-law Rakhi."

Rakhi was very sad to hear about the stroke and wanted to look after Ba. But, she had to obey Jogi's instructions and join the grandmother, Mani, who had a hard time running the house in Pinsad. Only when Devi arrived in Pinsad, Rakhi was sent to the estate to look after Ba.

Rakhi took the entire house work on her shoulders. She woke up at four in the morning to milk the cows and make butter from the yoghurt; it was a process carried out using a simple machine with a handle and a large beater. It was inserted in a large earthen pot containing yogurt and water. A worker would turn the handle to and fro for a long time in order to whisk the contents to form curd. The latter was then boiled to turn it to butter. She prepared breakfast for the workers and the children, and got the children ready for school. She cleaned the floors in the house and the kitchen with the help of a young female worker. Then, she would do other household work like preparation of snacks, washing and ironing of the bed sheets and the clothes, providing luncheons for the kids and Ba and attending to any problems relating to the farming activities. Ba provided the necessary advice as she knew best how Dinesh liked to conduct the business. Children became a slight burden on occasions for Rakhi as they relied entirely upon her presence when they were at home. However, Rakhi enjoyed their company tremendously but her health was neglected in pursuing all these activities. She had very little time for herself. She went to bed at midnight and sometimes very late when the children had lessons to do.

Then, one day, to her delightful surprise, she received Rahul's first letter. It was handed to her by the eldest son of Dinesh, Suresh who always anticipated the arrival of the postman at ten o'clock in the morning. Rakhi went to Ba's room where Ba was resting. She shut the door of the room. There were three beds in the room. There was no ceiling above all the rooms to avoid air circulation problem. The roof was low due to the prohibitive cost of timbers at the time the house was built. The roof consisted partly of the corrugated metal sheets and partly of wood.

"Ba, I got your son's first letter." Rakhi announced excitedly as she helped Ba to sit up.

"Let me know how he is and what he writes." Ba said as she rested her head on the high pillows.

When Rakhi opened the letter, Ba could see the glittering glow in her eyes. There was a roller coaster of gentle smile and shyness on Rakhi's face. She quickly looked at the handwritten address on the envelope and ran her fingers over the stamps. She blew in one corner of the envelope to insert her small finger to open one side slowly. She scanned the writings and went on explaining about Rahul's room, food, clothing, and views on the snow, friends and his health. Thus, having disclosed the relevant general news, she asked Ba's permission to read the letter in private. Ba suggested that she read it in her room as she felt that Dinesh had arrived. Rakhi sat in a corner and began to read the letter.

NOW I AM SO FAR AWAY

'Dear Queen of my heart, Rakhi,

Allow me to express my first sincere feeling for you by addressing you as the Queen of my heart. Also, please accept my apology for writing after almost three months. I have been confused about many things such as finding accommodation, school and the type of study, friends etc. Being a total stranger, it has been very difficult for me to settle here in the strange town. The biggest worrying concern was about the arrangement of the money for my existence. There were many obstacles in arranging the finance from Mozambique due to the political situation that we all know about. Anyhow, all that is over and I can relax and dream.

When we are alone, what else can we do but have dreams. I have many dreams. I reside in the dream world here. Life is totally lonesome, unattractive and strange. There is nothing around me to make me feel happy. Aloneness and isolation are the true hell. How artificial my life has become. I don't know how I am surviving in this land. When we found each other, we made life as real life in the short period of time and brought a little happiness and some tears in our lives. Meeting only you was enough for me; what more could I wish for in my life?

Let us make our newly found love life the ultimate thing to be cherished by exchanging letters. That way, our loneliness will not be so unbearable. Mind you, Dinesh could interfere in our life as he can read into my writings. Therefore, be careful not to let my letters fall in his, Devi's and cousins' hands. It will be a terrible disaster.

Let me now describe my life in this strange country. Before I came here, I had no idea where London was on the map. Although geography was my favourite subject in the New Era High school in Bombay, I concentrated on the Indian topography more for the purpose of passing the Secondary School Certificate examination. By the way, I am not in favour of conditional things in life. But, I have to accept all that for survival!

It is extremely cold here. I never experienced this type of murky weather. The cold crispy air I experienced in Massuri, the town located on top of a mountain near Himalayas, was very pleasing. However, it is beautiful to look at the knee deep snow. The trees appear dead, there being hardly any leaves on the branches. There are green shrubs, some with bright red 'berries' like tiny BOR fruits we find on farms. I spotted a beautiful bird with a red chest. I have never seen anything like that before. On Sundays and holidays, the roads are empty of people and vehicles. There is absolute silence that I can't bear, having spent time in buzzing Bombay. It enhances my loneliness and I wish you were here. Sometimes, I see children and dogs coming out late in the afternoon to play in the snow.

In the severely cold weather, I would feel less cold if you were with me. Each morning, I leave the world of dreams as I wake up. Soon after I finish making the bed, I think if only you were here with me. I would have asked you to do the bed. I know you wouldn't say no. I dream that as you approach the bed, I would grab you from behind and give a kiss on your cheek and ask,

"Rakhi, are you bored?"

When the cooking oil gets hot and I put some spices in a pot to make vegetable curry, hot mustard seeds fly out of the pot and land on my hand. They are painfully hot. I then realise that you must be going through this kind of process everyday, often burning your hands and sari. I thought that cooking was an easy task for all women. I realise now how wrong I was.

I dreamt once about you getting burnt and crying out loud. As I normally sit opposite you in the kitchen, I quickly came near you and asked,

"Now, let me see, how bad the burn is"

You showed your arm which I held and said,

"Oh, no" and immediately I kissed the area near the burn marks. You then pulled your hand off me, saying,

"Stop fussing around. Don't you have some work to do?" Your face was serious.

"OK boss, I will stem my overflowing love for you." I then go away.

Here is another of my dreams last night,

'It was a night in our village. After supper, I sat outside the front door of the house till eleven; then I made my way slowly up the stairs to the bedroom. I shut the door very quietly so that you wouldn't be disturbed from your sleep. I came near the bed and observed that your uncovered feet were off the bed. In the faint golden light, thrown by the lantern and the cool breeze, blowing through the bedroom window, your hair curls were swaying like the stems of the rice plants. There was a serene look on your face. I stared at your face for a while before leaning down on to your lips for a kiss. I whispered,

"Rakhi"

You were startled at first but soon consoled yourself seeing my face.

"Feeling very sleepy, are you?"

"No" you said in half sleep.

"You cheat. OK, so you go to sleep but cover yourself properly. Just look at you, is that how you sleep?" I murmured as I covered you. I was concerned about you catching cold. Then, suddenly you opened your eyes and said,

"I got tired of waiting for you and fell asleep. What were you doing sitting outside the house?

"OK, tomorrow I will announce to the others that my Rakhi awaits my presence. Will that do?"

"Oh, go away. I am not saying anything" you said as you were turning your face away. However, you were in my grasp and couldn't turn as I laid a kiss on your lips.

"Rakhi, am I niggling you too much?"

You said nothing.

"Say something, darling"

You covered your face with your hands. I slowly moved your hands away and said,

"Moon can't be covered up. You know that. The clouds come and float away soon". I, then, tried to cover you with blanket but you said,

"Don't bother, I will cover myself"

"Why, don't you like it if I cover you? OK by me."

I went to my bed next to yours. I turned my back towards you and tried to sleep. Suddenly, you jumped on my back. You touched my cheek and kissed me and said,

"Felt bed, uh?"

I turned my body to grab you and turned you towards the right side of the bed and whispered,

"Rakhi, do you want to stay in my house?"

"What do you mean your house?"

"Well, this bed is my house. I also believe that your bed is my house too." As you understood the meaning, you hid your face into my chest. Later, you came near my ear and whispered,

"So you can't wait today, uh?"

"Wait for what?"

"Don't ask me". Again, you hid your face in my chest. I lifted your face and asked,

"Rakhi, I don't understand"

"Don't be so naïve". I soon realise what you were trying to tell me. I whispered to you,

"Oh, no Rakhi, I haven't thought of it today"

"Then, why did you invite me from my house?"

"Not for what you are thinking. I just wanted to fall asleep, cuddling you. That way I have a sweet sleep and fall in love with you. I always want to stay near you. That is why I called you. Hang on a bit; I didn't call you in the first place. You came to me, remember?"

"So, you are not so keen, then?"

"Oh, I have been keen from that day" I looked into your eyes.

"Remember, we slept together for the first time at midnight in Bombay?"

"You told me then that you were not interested at all"

"You are right. If I could have stayed with you, then I wouldn't have said so".

You remained silent for a while. I thought you were falling asleep. I squeezed you gently. I was tempted to have the intimacy with you, but you spoke shyly,

"Not now. Next time whenever you would say, I would"

It was well past the midnight. After prolonged kisses, we fell in deep sleep.'

'In the following morning, you went downstairs early and came back with my toothbrush etc. You slowly opened the bedroom door and came to my bed and sat near me. You brought your face near mine and kissed my lips and said,

"Wake up"

You covered my yawning mouth as I stretched my arms. I got hold of your arm and braced it to my chest and tried to sleep again. You bent down as I pulled your arm.

"Is the thought not over yet?" you began to say.

"No" I said as I played with your hair curl. Then looking straight into your eyes, I said,

"Rakhi, I want to rape you." I was jokingly showing you my male supremacy and keen infatuation.

"Oh yeh, let's see, go on, try", you challenged.

I quickly pulled you to my right despite your resistance. My lips fell on yours. You were forced to give in. But, you appeared to be breathless.

"Rakhi, are you tired?" Motionless, you stayed on my chest. After a while, you got up and said,

"Come on, let's go"

"Will you bathe me?"

"You are not a two years old baby that I have to bathe you".

"So, you would bathe the little ones only, is that it?" I saw a little anger on your face.

Before you could attack me, I began to run towards the door, but you caught me.

"OK, OK, boss, so I lost". Then, both walked, our hands on the shoulders, near the stairs. You went downstairs first. I followed you a little later. The members of our family are strict about husband and wife coming down hand in hand. It looked disrespectful to the elders.

At lunch time, as there was no one about, I said,

"Shall I feed you, Rakhi?"

"Don't be silly. What if someone sees us?"

"You never mind that. Today, I must insist that you eat a little from my hand."

I half got up and stretched out my hand with food towards your mouth. You were annoyed. But, I still tried to put the food in your mouth. You reluctantly accepted. I returned to my place to finish eating. When you returned to the room at night, you got horrified to see my finger bandaged. You queried, holding my hand,

"What happened?"

"Nothing"

"No, tell me, how did this happen?"

"A slight cut"

"How, when?"

"As I was feeding you at lunch time"

"How could you cut your finger when you were feeding me?" You wondered.

"In your anger, you perhaps weren't aware of the knife in your hand"

You became nervously silent. You began to rub my hand gently and said,

"I am sorry, forgive me"

"Would you do the same to me for feeding you forcefully?" You hugged me but said nothing.

"Today, I will take you to my house. Will you come?" You said.

"It is very far"

"I will carry you, shall I?"

"Then I will come" But before you try to take me into your arm, I lifted you and said,

"Tell me, where is your 'house'?"

"There is no need to tell an angel".

We reach your 'house'. You laid flat on your back but I remained seated on the bed.

"Why are you still sitting?"

"You are lying down, aren't you? That is good enough for me."

"Now what?"

"I am thinking of an event. Before I tell you about it, you must promise me that you will not doubt about my relationship with a girl in Bombay, OK?"

"Agreed"

"Then listen. When I was studying in Bombay at the age of fifteen, I met this girl with whom I established very close friendship. She was very attractive. We attended the same private school in Bombay. We were taken to the school by the bus that collected various students living in different parts of the central Bombay. We weren't in the same year of study. The girl was invited to our flat in the Church gate C road. Devi aunty suspected that I was going too far with this girl. To her, I seemed to talk about the girl many times during a day. She disclosed her opinion to Dinesh uncle and both conspired to think of my marriage. Now you know how I got married to you".

I saw your peaceful face starring at me. I understood your dilemma.

"Look Rakhi, this sort of friendship is made by every young person. I didn't do any wrong. But, now that you have come into my life, I don't look at any other girl. I didn't mention about this to you during our pre-wedding days because it would have created doubts in your mind".

"Where is she?"

"In Bombay"

"Will you take me to her?"

"Of course, I will if she is still there. Why, you still have doubts about me? I give you her address, if you like".

"No, I trust you."

I bowed a little towards you and put my hand over your head and said,

"Rakhi, I wouldn't think of anyone else but you. You are my soul". I put my head over your chest.

"Go to sleep. Why do you worry so much like this?"

"I like to worry about you".

"Alright then, you do that".

I slowly lowered myself partly over you and asked you,

"Can I sleep over you like this?"

You said nothing.

"I suppose you will get tired, uh?"

"No" You held me with your one hand.

"I know you say no but you will get tired."

There was no answer from you. We both fell asleep.'

Alas, that was the dream last night. Now I am thinking about my lunch. But, what do I know about cooking, Rakhi? The shops are closed. I think I will open up a small tin of baked beans and eat with buttered bread and mango pickle.

My darling, I don't want you to worry about me. I have been sent here as a founding father to set an example for the others. We will have life of our own, away from Dinesh and his crowd. You look after yourself and mother and keep writing to me so that I could get your affectionate moral support in order to survive in this strange place. Love you. Yours Rahul.'

P.S. Please take good care of Ba. She must be feeling very lonely without me and father. Tell her that I think of her everyday and love her very much.'

RAKHI, THE FIRST EXPERIENCE

There was a lingering chill in the early hours of that December '55 morning. Rakhi sat on the edge of the backyard. She was shivering and crying. Through the tears in her eyes, all that she could see was the hazy glow of the burning fire in the nearby field. The fire burning inside her heart was unbearable. The first rape by Dinesh was a traumatic experience for her.

Meera was busy preparing early morning tea in the kitchen for all the people on the estate. She heard the faint sound of crying. She hurried towards Rakhi and put her hand on her head and said,

"What is it Beti? Why are you sitting here crying?"

Rakhi's mouth became very dry. She trembled. Fear of her future made her speechless. She tried to wipe her tears as she said:

"Nothing."

"Come now, you are going to catch cold here, we must go inside the kitchen."

She helped Rakhi to get up, and then both walked inside the kitchen. Meera offered her hot tea and told her to sit on the tall stool near the fire. Meera moved in front of her and asked:

"What is the matter Beti? Has someone told you off? Tell me, I will sort it out."

Rakhi shook her head and said:

"No one has told me off, Ba". She referred to Meera as Ba.

"Then why the tears?"

Rakhi looked at her and like a baby she burst into tears. Meera hugged her and said,

"Shuuush, do not cry my baby. Tell me what happened."

"Last night, he crept up suddenly near my bed and climbed over me quickly and did to me what he did to you. I tried to escape from him but

59

he was too powerful. He put his hand over my mouth. I could not cry for help. I am shaking all over. Ba, what is going to happen to me?" She dug her head onto Ba's chest.

Tears rolled down from Ba's eyes. She remembered how Dinesh raped her soon after her husband, Govind, died. Rahul was eleven years old. Meera, Reena, Rahul, and Rakhi became the responsibility of Dinesh, the younger brother of Govind. The only regret Dinesh showed was to say to all in the family,

"My brother was the guiding light like that of the moon of the 2nd day. It is now dented." Two didn't look alike the same; Govind was taller and had an oval shaped darker brown face whereas Dinesh was short and had a round brown face.

Meera had no one to turn to. In any case, no one would believe her story. However, but for her young children, Rahul and Reena, she would have committed suicide to end all the cruelties inflicted upon her by Dinesh, which went on until Rakhi came into Rahul's life. Dinesh made Meera and Rakhi responsible for cooking and entertaining visitors, to see that all work in the house and on the farms was carried out properly in time and to pay the wages every evening. If something went wrong, Dinesh swore at them openly and insulted both in the presence of the workers on the estate. The others in the family knew how hot tempered Dinesh was.

Meera hugged Rakhi, stroked her head, and said:

"I know how you must be feeling, Beti. There, there, my girl, shush now."

Meera managed to control her tears and looked up and said:

"Oh my Lord, give this girl the strength she needs now. We know that we mortals must refine the impurities within us by our KARMA so that we could be with you eventually." She then looked at Rakhi and said,

"When I was your age, my mother told me that there would be many hurtful events in one's life. You must not be frightened of them. We must continue with life's KARMA."

Rakhi's understanding of Karma was that whatever work was to be performed in her life, irrespective of resultant pain or happiness, was predestined. She must continue doing it in the present life. She knew that if her Karma was evil involuntarily, be it in this life or in the previous one, she must regret and pay the price for it.

Meera wiped her tears, held her at a short distance away, and said:

"Try avoiding him as much as possible. I know that he is a dictator of all things in this house. I will try to see that you are nowhere near the devil. Have you been hurt badly?"

Rakhi dug her head into Meera's chest again, implying that she was unhurt. After bathing, Rakhi ate some food. She was to sleep in Ba's room from that day onward.

Before Rahul left for England, Rakhi promised that she wouldn't write a single complaint to him. She didn't write about the rape for fear that he would believe Dinesh and not her; in any case, it was always the fault of the woman in such a situation. She feared the consequences if she did report it, such as divorce and discredit for her parents, brothers and sisters and her future. Thus, if she had reported pregnancy to her parents, the whole of her family would have faced a great tragedy. As people in Sakri and other villages held high regards for Bhima family for their adherence to the principle of credibility and culture, they would turn against them for the shameful act brought about by Rakhi. Rakhi's plea for mercy based on the disclosure of forceful rape by Dinesh wouldn't have been accepted by the society in which it was considered that a woman was at fault. Also, Dinesh would have lost his image in his family. He could have faced a court action. However, Rakhi's parents could have tried for a private abortion keeping the news secret and a divorce would have resulted much against the wish of Rakhi.

DINESH, THE DICTATOR

He created a big estate out of a virgin soil in a remote village in the district. Dinesh had invested a vast fortune belonging to the family in Africa. Govind had the ability to determine a good investment and worked very closely with Dinesh. Govind was an honest person. Dinesh was a short necked, chubby, selfish, power hungry and adventurer. On many occasions, both had disagreements over business policies. Whilst in Africa, Dinesh insisted on exporting bananas with other producers to the German market for the first time. Govind was against the policy. He said,

"Because it is a new market for us, I think the risk involved is great. I don't think the others have realised it."

"The agent who has organised the scheme knows what he is doing. The others have been informed about the prospect of good return" said Dinesh.

"What did the agent say? Did you personally hear him?"

"I didn't hear him but asked Mr Lalvani about it. As you know, he is expert on the rules and regulations about export business. His brother has joined the scheme. So there should be no fear of losing money. I think we should send our bananas."

Govind deliberated as he looked at Dinesh and then said,

"Go ahead if you want to. I believe we should stick to our South African customers. We have been trading with them for years. They are trustworthy customers. How would they feel when they find out that we will not be able to send bananas to them?"

"I think we will get lot more money from Germany than we would get from South Africa."

In the end, Dinesh won like so many ideas in the past he had won.

However, the expected money never materialised. The customs authority in Germany didn't allow the goods due to the unacceptable paperwork.

The agent disappeared overnight and the farmers made a great loss. After Govind's death, Dinesh took charge of everything affecting the family.

Dinesh was married to Devi, Meera's younger sister. It was an arranged marriage. At first, Dinesh was engaged to Meera and he liked her much. However, the parents, Jogi and Mani decided that their elder son Govind should marry to the elder sister Meera and the younger son Dinesh should marry Devi. Despite protest from Dinesh, his father told him to marry Devi. He had no choice. The parents followed the traditional rule that the elder son married to an elder sister when two sisters were marrying into the same family.

Dinesh was of a whimsical nature. He had no history of being cruel to women. However, he began to treat women as house furniture to be used as and when he wished. At the earliest opportunity, he would establish relationship with a woman of his desire; then pursue her until he succeeded in having an intimate relationship. After the death of Govind, he raped Meera whom he had wanted to marry. She felt helpless; she was not in the position to complain to anyone. It was considered her fault in the society that she submitted herself to the situation. His beady eyes turned to Rakhi too. He seriously believed that Rakhi needed a man's company in the absence of Rahul because she was a matured woman.

As the head of the family, Dinesh could resort to violence to stop both women disclosing the rapes to others. Once, he threw a broken sharp piece of slate in the face of school teacher and walked out of the school for good. He was hot tempered and swore frequently. He would fabricate, be cruel and take revenge against anyone who disagreed with him. He feared only the serious encounters of his action which could damage his credibility in the society. He was a representative head of a political party in his district. A young person was murdered during a public meeting held before the general election. Dinesh was appointed as the chairperson. An argument arose about party polices between the man and his opponent. They voted for their respective parties which were in fierce competition to win the seat in the district. The argument escalated to physical violence. Amidst the general public mayhem, the young person was murdered. The police department made Dinesh responsible for the incident. Dinesh hid away for many weeks. His son, Suresh bribed the lawyer to reducing the criminal charge to a lower level. The end result was that Dinesh spent two nights in the local jail.

Dinesh and Devi had two sons, Suresh and Anil. Devi was thin, illiterate and lazy. She had deep black eyes and dark complexion. She wore an oversized sari as she liked to wrap it twice around her waist. She had her own ways to do everything as she wanted. If she made a mess of cooking or gave money to her sons without the knowledge of Dinesh, Meera covered up her mistakes to protect the credentials of their parents. Devi always made sure that her elder sister did her work. Devi was pregnant several times after the birth of Anil but in every instance, she had a miscarriage. She was about forty-five years old when Rahul got married.

Devi suspected that Rahul might form a very close relationship with a girl of different caste during his school days in Bombay. The school bus collected children from the Marin drive area in the morning and brought them back home in the evening. Devi used to look out of the lounge window to see Rahul getting out of the bus. One day, she saw a girl getting out with Rahul. They frequently laughed as they talked for some time. When Rahul came in the flat, Devi asked him,

"That was a nice looking girl you were talking to downstairs. Who is she?"

"She is in my class."

"Does she travel with you in the bus every day?"

"Yes." Rahul began to suspect aunt's motive.

"Why don't you invite her here for a snack tomorrow?"

"I will tell her"

The girl, Mayuri entered the flat and greeted Devi with Namaste on the following evening. Devi asked her to take a seat and said,

"Delighted to see you; thank you for coming today. Would you like a cold drink?"

"No thanks." Mayuri was shy and kept looking at Rahul who sat on a chair near her.

"What is your name?" asked Devi.

"Mayuri"

"Oh that is a lovely name. I have prepared a snack. I will be here in a minute."

As Devi was making her way towards the kitchen, Mayuri got up and followed her.

"Oh, you don't have to come. I can manage. Please sit with Rahul and talk to him. Mayuri turned towards Rahul who smiled and winked at her indicating with his arm to join him. Devi managed to see the last bit of

Rahul's action as she brought out a tray with three plates of food. Mayuri turned and tried to take the tray from Devi's hands.

"Oh no, please, you sit down and start eating the snack while I get some drinks."

Devi went inside the kitchen and came out quickly with orange juice for all. As she took her seat she stared at Mayuri and said,

"Do you live locally?"

"Yes, in Kiran Mahal, Churchgate A Road."

"Where are you originally from?"

"Kathiawad, Saurastra, Utter (North) Gujarat"

"Are you Brahmin?"

"Yes. My mummy and papa migrated to Bombay before I was born."

"What do they do now?

"We have our diamond business."

Devi squinted and rolled her eyes giving a disapproving look to Rahul. He immediately understood that he should not associate with Mayuri. He said,

"Aunty, we travel together in the school bus but she is in a different class in the school. Her friends are my friends too. The teachers keep us very busy, isn't that so Mayuri?"

Devi got up and picked up the empty plates and made her way into the kitchen. She gestured Rahul to join her.

"Son, don't get involved with her too much. We are Patel and she is Brahmin. Our ways of life are very different than theirs. People will talk about us if they see you with her every day." said Devi. Rahul didn't like her inference. He unenthusiastically said,

"OK, I will see to that."

He walked hastily towards Mayuri and sadly said,

"Come, your parents must be wondering why you haven't been at home by now. Let's go downstairs."

Mayuri realised that Rahul was upset. As they were going down, she said,

"Did your aunt tell you something to upset you?"

Rahul couldn't help telling her; he stopped and looked straight into her eyes as he said,

"Mayuri forgive me for telling you to leave so soon. She said that we shouldn't continue to meet because people might think that we are in love. Please don't conclude that I don't like you. You are my best friend. I admire your smile and the sweet voice. I hope that we will continue our friendship." Rahul looked down sadly. She held his hand and said,

"Look up to me, Rahul. I understand your aunt's viewpoint. This doesn't mean we can't remain as friends. Of course, we will meet every day because I like your individuality and thoughts. If I may say so, you are handsome too. So, don't be sad. All you have to bear in mind that you don't speak about me in your house."

Rahul smiled and thanked her.

Devi pursued her thought relentlessly to convince Dinesh that Rahul should get married soon. When Dinesh came to the flat, Devi informed him about her observation of Rahul and Mayuri meeting everyday in the school bus. She said,

"I invited her one day and found out that Rahul, from his behaviour seems to like her. She is of Brahmin cast. I told Rahul to stop meeting her. They still travel together in the school bus. Rahul is sixteen years old and I think we should consider his marriage. Can you imagine what the people would say when they find out that our son is married into a Brahmin family?"

Dinesh simply said to Rahul,

"I hope that you are studying hard for the forthcoming matriculation examination. Don't waste your time after other things."

Rahul realised that aunty had words with Dinesh about Mayuri. To Meera, Rahul was a sentimental and clever son. She was denied to fulfil her desire to keep Rahul with her all the time knowing that Dinesh suppressed her son's ideas in every respect. Dinesh knew that Rahul was intelligent but Dinesh objected anyone who undermined his authority. Devi could see the opportunity for getting a credit if she could persuade her husband to get Rahul married. She resorted to the same trickery when involved in affairs of her relatives and friends.

Dinesh's son, Anil with dark brown face and black eyes was a squanderer; soon he demanded money from Rakhi to spend on food items and soft fizzy drinks from a local shop. He knew that Rakhi's aunt sent money to her regularly. Rakhi gave him the money to avoid any hassle that she might encounter from him. Anil took advantage of his right, by virtue of Rakhi being married to his elder cousin, to ask for anything from her.

He approached boldly towards Rakhi,

"If you don't give me the money, I will tell my father that you refuse to give money. I don't think you will like what he could say to you. Moreover,

I will tell my friends that you are very miserly and during Holi time we will gang up against you and spray some thick oil based mixture of colours."

Rakhi feared Anil's look. She was only fourteen but had the sense to foresee a danger coming from Anil who was nine years old.

Dinesh was having many disagreements with his wife over having more children. He was eager to have a frequent sexual relationship. Every time he tried to have sex with her, she pleaded,

"Not tonight please. I feel tired of having miscarriages. I am very tired tonight."

Dinesh got very upset and forced his way to conclude the entry into her. She tried to push him away but he slapped her hard as he forced himself deep into her and ejaculated. Soon he dumped his heavy body on her and lay there for some time. She tried to roll him over from her but he was too heavy. She often cried when she found out that she was pregnant. Dinesh realised that she wasn't going to give him good sex as the time passed by. So he looked elsewhere for satisfaction of his carnal desire. He found Meera first. Then, his beady eyes turned towards Rakhi who became the easy prey.

One hot afternoon, he coaxed a young female farm worker to a storage house to have sex with her. She was beautiful with wide eyes and had voluptuous busts and a broad smile. Dinesh hand held her and gently pushed her towards the door of the house. Every worker knew the fearful nature of Dinesh. No one would dare to interfere with his activity.

Unfortunately, his younger brother Rana's son, Amrit came to pick up some equipment kept in the storage house. As he opened the door, he witnessed Dinesh copulating with a girl on the floor. He shut the door quickly. Dinesh had called him for some help on the farm. Dinesh had realised that Amrit saw him with the girl. When Dinesh finished raping, the girl was crying and said to him,

"I will tell my father that you forcefully raped me."

Dinesh swore and said,

"You silly bitch, you enjoyed it, didn't you? What more do you want? Here, I give you some money you would never earn in a year. You are good and if you need any more help come to me."

She hesitated taking the money thinking that it was dirty money. However, considering that the family lived at below subsistence level, she took the money and hastily walked out of the place.

One year later, she came to the farm house in the morning to show Dinesh his son. Several workers picked up equipments and walked out towards farms without noticing the events happening around the front of the house. In any case, they wouldn't hang around where Dinesh was present.

"I thought that you may want to see your son." The mother said in a quiet low voice as she neared Dinesh.

Dinesh was petrified seeing his baby son who had similar facial features to his. He didn't touch the boy. He looked around to see if anyone was present. But for a female worker in the front lounge cleaning the furniture, he saw no one else. He said,

"You stupid woman, did you have to bring him here? Don't you bring the baby here ever again, do you understand me?" He gave her money and told her to go away for good.

Although he knew that Amrit wouldn't dare to disclose his act to others, he inherently feared that disclosure would harm his credibility in the society and in the family. From that day, he acted favourably towards Amrit who was 14 years old and who feared Dinesh. However, Dinesh never missed the opportunities to cheat and defame him and his father, Rana subsequently. One day, while he sat on a chair near the desk, he looked into the account book of the estate. Rana came to seek a favour of his elder brother.

"How are you?" said Dinesh as he looked at Rana.

"Fine." Rana sat on the swing hung outside the main entrance to the house.

Meera came out of the house with water for Rana.

"How are you Bhabhi (Sister-in-law)?" asked Rana as he drank water.

"I am well. How is Bijliben?"

"She is fine. She remembered you and invited you to join her in Pinsad." Bijliben was Rana's wife.

As Meera went inside the house, Dinesh shut the account book and asked,

"Why is this sudden visit here? Are things OK at home?"

"Everything is fine. It's just this problem that cropped up unexpectedly It is about the insurance premium on my policy. They want 2000 rupees and I don't have that much money. What with the purchase of fertiliser and a few other things for the mango trees and sugarcanes recently I have run short of cash. So, perhaps you can give me the money for a short period of time." Rana anxiously looked at Dinesh.

Meera was standing behind the door to listen to the conversation. Dinesh noticed her presence and told her to prepare for lunch. Dinesh turned towards Rana,

"Look, I am also in the same situation. I have no surplus money. I was just looking into the accounts book to see where all the money had been spent. I have to tighten the outgoing of money from now. You should do the same thing. It is no use coming here without prior notice for the money you require." Dinesh drew hard on his cigarette.

"But, I didn't anticipate that the insurance company would give me a final warning. I tried to obtain money from the others but you know that people don't keep such large amount of money in their houses. If I don't pay now, my insurance will be terminated."

"Lunch is ready" said Meera.

"What can I do about the money now? I borrowed rupees 3000 from Raghuji last week. I now have to pay it at the end of this month." Dinesh said as he got up to enter the house for lunch.

"Brother, I have to catch the train in a half an hour. I am going now." Rana said as he stood up from the swing and prepared to walk away in disgust.

"You're not going without having lunch, are you? Have you felt bad over what I said about the money?"

"I am not hungry. I must catch the train on time otherwise the next one will be two hours later. I will ask Dhiraj in Navsari for the money." Rana walked away.

Dhiraj couldn't help Rana. Disappointed and angry, Rana told his son, Amrit to sell the car and pay the premium. Rana used his father's bicycle for the subsequent two years to conduct the business. He vowed that he wouldn't ask Dinesh for any favour again.

CENSORSHIP AND THE
DEATH OF MEERA

Rakhi wrote to Rahul as regularly as she could; He also kept in touch with her. Dinesh began to censor all the correspondence from Rahul. He read all the letters arriving at the estate and at Pinsad, his father's place. He disclosed some contents to his wife. Rahul wrote about his intense desire for being with Rakhi. He mentioned delirious state of his mind due to hard work with 'failure' results in the exams. He roamed in parks for hours thinking whatever he did would end in failure. He blamed himself for his lack of the knowledge of English vocabulary. He was taught primarily in Gujarati in which he was educated hitherto. He wrote that he wasn't interested in doing accountancy subject as Dinesh had wanted him to pursue. He was disheartened by his first failure in the English language examination.

The advice and criticism that Rahul got subsequently from Dinesh indicated to him clearly that something was wrong. The letters he got from Rakhi didn't contain references to certain questions put to her. Some letters were not passed on to Rakhi. He stopped writing and waited for a reaction from Rakhi.

Dinesh and Devi began to spread rumours that Rahul seemed to be spending more time with a girl and not concentrating on his study. Dinesh explained his thoughts to Devi about what Rahul could be doing in England. He said,

"I think he is spending money after films and other leisure activities with his friends. He has a bad company of friends. Some of them live with English families and possibly have girlfriends. Others may be the sons of rich parents in Africa. We don't have that kind of money to squander. Rahul has to study hard and learn English properly to get the degree in accountancy field. Who knows, he may have an English girlfriend already. That would be a disaster for all of us. Perhaps, he would never think of returning to India to take over the accounts side of the estate business. We will have to do something about him. I will inform my father and Rakhi's parents about this. There could be a possibility of divorce."

Devi interjected,

"In our family, we never have had a divorce before. It would look bad if Rahul is to divorce Rakhi. Both parents would disagree to the idea. How would we arrange another marriage for Rahul? As you say, he might not come back after the divorce and get married to his English girl friend."

Dinesh was concerned more of his fear that should Rakhi disclose about the rapes, he would be discredited badly in the society. He grabbed the opportunity to spread the rumours about Rahul. No one else knew about his rapes to Rakhi except Meera. When Rakhi heard about the rumours, she got worried and desperately wrote letters to Rahul. But there were no replies from Rahul. Jogi noticed Rakhi's depressed mood. He asked his wife Mani to find out the reasons for it.

"Rakhi beti, come and sit next to me. I want to know something".

"Be with you in a minute, Ma"

"No, leave everything you are doing and come here please".

She came and sat next to Mani who looked at her and said,

"You look very tired. Are you OK?"

"Yes"

"Have you eaten today?"

"Yes Ma." Rakhi looked down.

"If you can't handle the work, leave it. No one is going to tell you off. We have many servants to do the work. I think you aren't taking care of yourself, am I right?"

Ma, looking at Rakhi, began to crack a small betel-nut with a special small cutter. Rakhi's tears began to fall on the floor. Mani touched the side of her face and softly said,

"Tell me beti, what is it?"

"Ma, he has stopped writing to me. I haven't had a single reply to my letters for many weeks. Dinesh uncle and Devi aunty are saying that he is spending time with a woman."

Mani wiped her tears and pulled her close and said,

"Don't worry, your grand dada will find out soon about it. You must eat properly from now on. I am sure Rahul must have a good reason for not writing. We will find out. Leave all the work to the servants from now and you rest my child. Don't worry now."

Rakhi went upstairs to rest. Meanwhile Mani informed Jogi,

"Poor girl, she is worried to death because Rahul hasn't replied to her letters for a long time. Dinesh and Devi were saying that as Rahul failed in English language exam, it seems he could be spending time with a girl. My Rahul would never do such a thing. I am certain of it."

Mani was standing near the door of the lounge where Jogi was reading a daily newspaper. He raised his eyes slowly from the paper to look at Mani for a second. Then he said,

"Why didn't you tell me about what Dinesh and Devi were saying about Rahul?"

"Rakhi just told me."

Jogi put the paper on table as he got up and said,

"I am going to Navsari to make enquiries about Rahul. Meanwhile, if Rakhi wants to go to her father's then arrange to send her straight away. Don't tell Dinesh anything as he would make a fuss."

"I will send her this afternoon. Would you like to have tea before you go?"

"Yes. I think that is a good idea. Sudha makes very bad tea." Sudha was the wife of Jogi's best friend, Thakor who worked for the local council in Navsari.

Around four o'clock, Rakhi left for her father's village, Sakri. No sooner she had arrived in the house; to her extreme surprise she received a letter from Rahul. She was ecstatic and ran straight inside the house to Bhabhu and gave her a big hug.

"Oh my mad girl, what are you so happy about? When did you come? We didn't know about you coming here." Bhabhu grabbed Rakhi and ran her hands over her face.

"I just arrived here and was handed this letter by the boy servant."

Then, suddenly Bhabhu frowned; she said,

"Oh God, why are you so thin? Are you eating well? Is there any problem with your in-laws? Come sit on the swing, beti"

"Bhabhu, I had a problem that looks like its resolved now as soon as I stepped inside this house. See this letter; it came here just now from London after a long time. Rahul hadn't replied to my last few letters. Dinesh and Devi were saying that Rahul had a girlfriend. I was so worried but couldn't tell to Ba or Ma. I couldn't eat and sleep for days. There is so much work in the house and I can't cope with it. Ba knew the comments made regarding Rahul by others. She kept telling me that I shouldn't worry about him,

"My son wouldn't touch another woman" she said.

But, I couldn't help feeling sad about it. Then, after I told Ma, Jogidada went to Navsari and told Ma to send me here. I'm glad that I came here. Ba was pleased to see me go too."

Rakhi's father, Bhima was concerned when Rakhi spoke of the rumours about Rahul. He looked at Rakhi as he asked the reason for her sudden arrival.

"Hello Beti (Daughter), are you well? I am very pleased to see you. Is everything all right with you? Beti, I am very worried about the rumours. Tell me about Rahul," he said as he hugged Rakhi

"Bapa (Father), I am alright but I want to read the letter first and then I will tell you more."

As Rakhi decided to go to a bedroom upstairs, Bhabhu held her left arm and asked,

"Are you not having anything to eat first?"

"No".

She ran upstairs and locked the door before settling down to read the letter. The parents smiled as they saw her hurrying. Bhabhu said,

"That's my silly girl."

Rakhi opened the letter and found a small photo of Rahul tucked between the pages. There was a delightful smile on her pale face. She dumped herself on the bed and gave a kiss to the photo and said,

"Why did you take such a long time to write?" Then, hurriedly she began to read the letter.

"My Queen of the heart, Rakhi,

Once again, I offer my apology for the possible anxiety that I may have caused you. I am fine. I hope you are well too. I mentioned to you before to watch out for the censorship of letters by Dinesh and Devi. I wrote to you but wondered why I had no reply I expected one from you for a while. Then, I realised that my letters were being censored. From Dinesh's usual instructions about how to live in London and avoid women and wine, I could read, from his relatively revealing statements, that he had read my letters to you. He wrote at great length about how not to get involved in the Western life style. I must avoid associations with women and avoid eating non vegetarian food. I wrote very personal things about us in my letters. They must have had a field day reading that. I now feel embarrassed about it. So, to test this, I write this letter to you at your father's place. I hope you will be there. You must have worried often for not hearing from me. I am sorry if that is the case.

Every morning, I wake up and think of your gorgeous face which I try to keep in focus. In this foggy place, it is easy to lose the clarity of things. But I keep looking at your photograph and sometimes I talk to you!

'Hey, this is a miserable life here. It gets very cold. The heating is expensive and I have to cut down on spending on other things. They send me £50 every month from Mozambique. Sometimes, I like to see more than one film with my Gujarati friends. They came from Salisbury and Bulawayo in Rhodesia. We were students at the school in Andheri, Bombay. I wish you were here so that I would feel very happy and then could pay lot more attention to my study.'

That is what I say to your photograph. I say something different each time. When I had flu, I felt very lonely and miserable in bed for days. The Greek landlady is very kind and caring. The Greeks believe in a communal type of living, like ours. She gives me hot soup and bread toasts. One day, she said,

"Rul, you must drink a little brandy to get rid of your cold." She can't pronounce my name properly.

"Mum, I hate brandy; I don't like any alcoholic drinks. It's against my religion"

"Don't be silly, my boy. The medicine that the doctor has given to you contains alcohol. I say you take a small amount of brandy before going to bed as medicine."

"I will bear it in mind, mum".

I call her Mum because she is very much like our Ba. She often asks me about you and our family. I think I am very lucky to be with her here. Her son, Geoffrey and I go to the same college in London. He helps me with English.

How is your health? Are you eating well? I see from your recent photo you sent to me that you are looking very thin.

Please do look after yourself. If they are making you work hard at home, let me know so that I can tell them about your health. You might think that they will blame you for complaining to me. I am sure that Jogi dada will understand. Come to think about this, they must have told you often to leave the work to the servants and rest. When you are at your parent's house, try to go and see films in the city and visit shops. You are your uncle's favourite. Tell him to take you to see the places of interest. Be happy, my darling. I know you must be worrying a lot. I wish I could send you money, but what I have is barely enough to meet the cost of living here. Well, I must prepare for the forthcoming examination. Mum keeps an eye on me; she doesn't want me to go to cinemas and other places in London, not even in the YMCA where I practice badminton. Please pass my regards to everyone in the house. My next letter will be sent to the Pinsad address, hoping Dinesh wouldn't be able to get hold of it. Jogidada wouldn't open the letters addressed to you. Look after yourself and don't worry about me. Love you a lot. Rahul."

Rakhi came downstairs and spoke to Bhabhu and father,

"See Bhabhu, Rahul is OK. He is well looked after by a Greek lady whom he addresses as Mum because she is like Ba. She doesn't allow him to go to see films and other people because he is preparing for the examination. Bapa, he is well and I am not to worry about the rumours now. He sends his regards to you all. He has Gujarati friends. Geoffrey, Mum's son helps him with English."

Rakhi sat on the swing and closed her eyes for a moment. Bhabhu sat next to her and said,

"I am so happy to know that Rahul is well. I thank God for that."

Bhabhu wiped her tears as she held Rakhi's hand. She stroked Rakhi's head and kissed her on the forehead. Rakhi opened her eyes and looked at Bhabhu and said to her,

"You don't worry about anything now. Have you eaten?"

Bhabhu shouted at the servant to prepare the lunch.

One afternoon, Rakhi heard a car's hooting and at once recognised that the Ford saloon car had come from Pinsad. The car pulled up in front of the house. Bhima came out from the house and greeted the driver, who said,

"I have come to take Rakhi home. Meera Ba is seriously ill. Dinesh Sahib and Jogi dada said that Rakhi's presence was necessary."

Presently, Rakhi and Bhabhu came to the front door of the house. Upon hearing what the driver had said, Rakhi remembered that Meera was very sad and tearful when she left for Sakri. Rakhi thought that it was due to her leaving and Ba would have to look after everything. Rakhi knew that Meera wouldn't be able to cope with all the work. However, she decided, with tacit acceptance from Meera, to come to Sakri, So, Rakhi assumed that Meera must have missed her too much and sent for her return.

When Rakhi arrived at Pinsad in the afternoon, she saw many sad looking people gathered outside the house. Almost all of them wore white clothes, a sign of anticipated death. One lady said to Rakhi,

"Beti, your Ba is very ill. Go hurry"

She hurriedly moved into the house. It was hot inside the room. Some elder people from the village sat in the front room full of Bidi smoke. Rakhi's heartbeats increased as she approached Meera. Devi, with tears running down her face, held Rakhi's arm and escorted her to the bed. She saw Ba in bed surrounded by Dinesh, Vanoo, the son-in-law of the family, Devi and Mani. Presently, Dinesh moved away and joined the people in the front room. Meera was unconscious for several days. The family doctor had diagnosed that she had suffered a serious stroke, leaving her face deformed and speechless. Rakhi cried and hastily moved towards Meera. She curved down on to her face. She tried to lift Meera's head but couldn't manage. Her tears fell on Meera's face. She managed to say,

"Ba", as she put her face on Meera's chest and cried more. Devi pulled her away gently and took her to the kitchen where Reena was warming milk for Ba.

Dinesh came near the bed and tried to put a spoonful of lukewarm milk in Meera's mouth but she couldn't swallow it. Her tongue had gone inside near the throat. Devi wiped the excess milk off Meera's mouth. This was done when there is no doubt that a person is dying. Meera tried to turn her face towards Jogi and opened her mouth a little as if trying to say something. Jogi softly asked her,

"Do you want to see Rakhi? She is here."

Meera closed her eyes. Tears flowed down her cheeks. Rakhi came and stroked her head and managed to say,

"Ba, I am here. What has happened to you?" Her tears fell on Ba's face. Meera opened her eyes slowly and looked at Rakhi. She squeezed

Rakhi's hand slightly and tried to shake her head, suggesting Rakhi was not to cry. Then as Rakhi curved down to Meera's face, she could hear a faint gargling sound emitting from Meera's mouth. She put her ear to Ba's mouth and heard,

"Rahhhh . . ." As Rakhi pulled her tearful face away, Meera had taken her last breath. Her eyes closed permanently. She remembered Rahul at the end of her life. Dinesh walked hurriedly towards the bed and saw Meera resting for good. There were no tears in his eyes. He put his hand on Meera's head for the last time.

A place on the floor was selected to put her body. The area was sprinkled with Holy water from the river Ganges. Then, the sacred grass (Dabhdo) was scattered over the area before putting a white cloth on top of it. Mantras were chanted as the body was brought down to rest over the white sheet. All men had vacated the room. The ladies washed the body. Rakhi cried a lot as she helped to clean the body. The grandmother, Mani took her away from the scene and left her with Reena.

After the wash, the body was dressed in the finest white cotton sari and the matching blouse. Her forehead was marked with a yellow sandalwood dot. A small garland made of sandalwood was put around her neck. A small lamp with Ghee on stand was lit next to her head. The funeral took place two hours later. The workers from the estate were brought over by bus to attend the funeral. It was to be concluded as soon as possible due to hot weather that expedites the decay process of the body. Many people from the village and Sakri joined in to say farewell to the lady who had served the community members by providing clothes, money and food, despite her personal hardship. Her body was secured to a bamboo bed to which four coconuts were tied in each corner. Also, a small amount of rice and lentils, tied in a handkerchief, were put on the bed. The family men took her to the nearest place of cremation by the river. Traditionally, the ladies would attend her up to the front gate of the house only. When the men carrying the body faded away in the distance, the ladies returned inside of the house. They cried for the loss of Meera and their own folks who died in the past.

Rakhi was devastated because she loved Meera dearly and realised that now she would be unprotected from Dinesh. There was no one as trustworthy and loving as Meera. Now she had no one to turn to, except God, Jogi dada and Mani. Jogi arranged to send a telegram to Rahul informing him about the death of his mother.

On receipt of the telegram, Rahul wrote to Rakhi for the details of how his mother died.

MUM HELD THE LETTER

It was a dull, cold and wet late evening on Saturday in June1959. Rahul had just finished his college examination. Now he wanted to relax at home for a while before commencing further study in September. One of his favourite hobbies was cinematography and he decided to spend time in the Royal Photographic Society's library to read about it

Mum asked him to come downstairs. When he came, Mum, who wore a loose-fitting light blue three quarter length dress was stitching pieces of black and white fabric on the machine kept in her large kitchen. Her family migrated to England from Cyprus many years ago. They settled in the Elephant and Castle area of London where they established a restaurant. The two floors above the restaurant were used for residential purposes. The one immediately above the restaurant was occupied by her family. There were five small rooms for letting to students on the top floor. Rahul occupied the first room nearest to the stairs leading to the floor downstairs.

In Mum's kitchen, there was a small sofa in one corner and a small chair and a fridge near the window. One solitary high wattage bulb hanging down from the middle of the ceiling lit the room. Mum's eyesight was poor and the light was left on all the time she worked. She found it convenient to work in the warm kitchen as she suffered from arthritis. She cooked food for her husband, daughter, son and one grandson. Mostly she cooked Greek food.

Before he entered the kitchen, Rahul could smell the aromatic flavour of 'Kubebia', a concoction of rice and spiced mince meat wrapped in vine leaves, marinated in red wine. It was being cooked in the oven at a slow heat. A large clear glass bowl containing orange flavoured jelly with pieces of mixed fruits was put on the dining table. The walls were painted white.

"Hello Mum." Rahul greeted her.

As she handed a registered letter to him, she said,

"Hello Rul, come in. This letter came this morning."

She stopped working and looked at him.

"Thanks Mum." Rahul's hand trembled as he held the letter. His heart began to throb faster. It was from Rakhi.

"If you don't mind, can you read the letter here? This letter could be about your mum. My heart is beating fast because I am anxious to know what happened to her. When you finish reading, tell me about the news please."

"OK."

She got up, filled the kettle with water and put it on the gas ring.

He sat on a chair and looked at the envelope for a second. As he opened it, he could smell the aroma of sandalwood, used on the occasion. He gently pulled out a page of letter. He ran his finger over the letter and felt the roughness of the paper. He realised that she must have got hold of it from a note book. He began to read the letter. Rakhi's handwriting was beautiful.

'My dear king of the heart, Rahul,

I have sad news to give you. My heart is heavy as I write this letter. I hope you are reading this at home, preferably in Mum's presence.

Our 'BA' is no longer with us. She had a massive stroke attack some weeks ago. I was at Sakri. The granddad sent the driver for me. I was there for two days only and then the driver had come. He told my Bapa that I was to go to our house immediately. Then, he whispered that BA was very ill and my presence was essential. I packed all my things in one hold all.

When I arrived at home, I noticed the anxious faces of the village people who wore white clothes standing outside of our house. The uniform clothes indicated the imminence of death. It was a late afternoon. I became very nervous and hurriedly moved inside the house. I saw BA in a bed surrounded by the family members. Jogi dada and Mani ma stood at the foot of BA's bed. Devi aunty was crying standing near Mum's head. Dinesh uncle sat, smoking Bidi, with others in the front living room.

BA was unconscious for several days. The family doctor had diagnosed that she suffered a serious stroke that left her face deformed and speechless. I cried and ran hastily towards BA and bent down onto her face. I tried to lift her head but couldn't manage to do so. My tears fell on her face. I managed to say "BA" as I put my face on her chest and cried. The aunt pulled me away gently and took me to the kitchen where Reena was warming milk for BA.

After a while, I stood near a place in the kitchen from where I could see Dinesh uncle trying to put a spoonful of lukewarm milk in BA's mouth. She couldn't swallow it as her tongue had gone down near her throat. She turned her face towards Jogi dada and tried to say something but she couldn't say a word. Jogi dada softly asked her if she wanted to see me. BA closed her eyes. I went to her and stroked on her head and managed to say that I was present. I didn't know what was happening to her.

My tears fell on her face. She opened her eyes slowly. She looked at my face as she squeezed my hand and tried to shake her head, as if telling me not to cry. Then, as I bent down towards her face, I could hear a faint gargling sound emitting from her mouth. I put my ear to her mouth and heard 'Rah . . . . '

As I pulled my face away in shock, BA took the last breath.

Please, look after yourself. I know how much you love BA. The guide that showed us the vision of future life and how to achieve things has gone away forever. Stay with Mum and eat well. I know that you don't eat when you get worried. May God give her soul the eternal peace? I am now all alone. I fear having to look after your brothers and sisters and the house alone. I know that Mum will look after you. Give my regards to her. Take care and keep in touch. I am fine and I love you very much. I am yours forever, Rakhi.'

Lightning struck outside the window. Thunderous rain drummed on the roof. The heavy eyelashes full of tears began to rain on Rahul's legs. Mum went near him and put her hand on his shoulder and looking at his face she shook her head indicating not to cry.

With tears rolling down, Rhaul looked at her and said in the broken voice,

"We know that my BA is no longer on this earth. Mum, I miss her a lot. Rakhi is living alone in the family. Ba had a stroke and could not speak. You know, before she died she tried to say my name. Rakhi heard it."

Now Rahul started to cry loudly.

Mum pulled a chair near him and gave him a tissue. She said,

"Oh my poor thing, don't cry. I know how you miss her now. I am concerned about poor Rakhi. What will she do now? I hope she will be alright. Write to her to say that you are going to be fine. I am here to look after you. Give my regards and tell her to be strong and avoid unnecessary worries."

She got up to make tea.

The memories of Rahul's past life with his mother fleetingly passed by. He remembered how he accompanied his ill mother who had to consult the family doctor in Navsari, the nearest city, two and a half kilometers away.

'At the age eleven, I began to notice selfish motives of people. I lived in a village with fifty houses in the Gujarat district of India. The people lived communally and they adhered to the code of practice established since they migrated from the Punjab area. Originally, the ancestors were very poor. They had the opportunity to acquire reasonably cheap and in some cases free land pieces.

I was brought up by my grandparents, mother and aunts. The grandfather was the sole income earner supporting ten members of the family. He worked as a watch repairer in the city nearby. He leased a piece of land, large enough to grow variety of crops like cotton, wheat, rice and sugarcanes. He planted mango trees around the field. The members of the family slept on the ground which was painted with the cow dung. They placed mats, made from jute strands, on the floor and spread cotton sheets over them. A cotton bedspread was used to cover them. The night lights were made of tins with wicks and kerosene fuel. They had one meal a day, mainly in the evening. For lunch, they had any leftovers from the previous evening and sometimes roasted peanuts and savouries all made at home. Chapattis, made of wheat flour, were considered as luxury items. They were for the guests and for festival celebration times. I loved a chapatti with molasses but could not get it every day for my lunch at the village school.

My mother became ill with high temperature. It was expensive to call the family doctor from the nearby city as the money was not easy to come by from the agricultural produce. She was told to walk to the surgery in the city which was three kilometres from the village. Also, there was no money available for the transport. The grandmother had prepared a large basket, full of vegetables, Ghee and some sweetmeats for her daughter who lived in the city. Even at my young age, I realised the inconsideration given to my mother's health. A house servant put the basket on my mother's head. A word of warning was given by the grandmother,

"Be careful of the bus drivers. They drive very near the edge of the roads; you could get seriously involved in an accident and get hurt."

It was almost midday with the temperature of 37*C. I didn't have shoes or slippers. My mother wore a well used pair of slippers she got from her father. She was concerned about my feet.

"What happened to your shoes you wear when you go to the school?"

She was looking at my feet which I couldn't keep in one place due to hot dust on the road.

"It will be OK, Ba. Don't worry about me"

I was aware of her health. I was very annoyed about no money being given for the transport, but I didn't show my anger to mother. We left the house and walked about quarter of a kilometre in the burning dust and heat before getting near the tarmac road. A bus passed by with some passengers hanging outside. The flying dust filled our eyes and nostrils even though we were standing reasonably far away from the road. As we began to walk on the road, my feet were in pain due to the hot tarmac surface. My mother noticed it and decided to stop for a while under a shadowed area. There were many bushy trees casting shadows on the sides of the road. After a short rest, as we began to walk, another bus stopped near us.

"Do you want to come aboard? It's very hot." said the driver.

My mother looked at the driver first and then at me, and asked me, "Are you OK?"

Although my feet were sore, I said I was OK. My mother thanked the driver and indicated that we would walk. If we had taken the ride, we would have been expected to pay the fares otherwise the other passengers would make a big noise. A kilometre down the road, we faced a large pond with stagnant water which provided the perfect breeding ground for the mosquitoes. As we proceeded further from that place, I said,

"Ba, can we stop under that tree as my feet are getting hot?" I pointed at a large tree that reminded me of an incident which caused great pain to my right foot in the past. We stopped under the shadowed area for a while. I told her about the incident.

'I was on the way barefooted to attend the school in the city. My books were weighty and now and then I had to stop under a shaded area for a little respite. It was getting very hot. I began to walk towards it from this side. Then, I heard the sound of a bus approaching from behind. To avoid possible accident, I decided to run at full speed. I dropped a book on the middle of the road. As the bus passed me it created a big dust cloud. I ran hurriedly, only to find me stepping on to a large thorn which pricked right through between the big toe and the adjoining toe. I began to cry instantly. I pulled out the blood covered thorn carefully. I felt as if lot of blood oozed out. I tied the handkerchief around the foot and made my way to collect the book from the road. I could see my friend coming towards me.

"Hey, what happened to your foot?" He said as we sat on a large stone. He held up my foot to see how much damage was done. As I wiped the tears, I angrily said,

"Bloody thorn went right through my foot as I tried to move quickly here to avoid the oncoming bus."

The friend offered me help by carrying my books. I kept my left arm around his shoulder as I limped all the way to the school.'

My mother listened silently as I cited the past experience. Then, she ran her fingers through my hair and as she wiped the perspiration on my face, she said,

"In future, always listen for the sound of a bus before crossing the road. You shouldn't run because the bus driver can see you from far away on this stretch of the road. He will slow down the bus. The book could have been destroyed and your granddad would have been very crossed with you. The books are expensive; you know that, don't you? Anyway, why do you leave our house before your friend leaves his?"

"He goes to work with his father on their farm in the early hours of the morning. I don't want to be late because the art teacher punishes whoever comes late. You know Ba, do you remember that day when I returned home from the school with my fingers swollen? That was because that horrible teacher made me put my fingers on the edge of a drawer which was slammed hard with his foot. My fingers could have broken. My granddad was very annoyed and wrote something addressed to the principal. From then, the teacher gave me a nasty look only; he did not punish me. I was very frightened of him at first".

"Alright my darling, let's make our way to the doctor."

I tried to help her to put the basket on her head.

At the surgery, after examining my mother, the doctor said that after the completion of the course of medicine, she must report back for an x-ray of her kidney. He emphasised that she shouldn't walk to his surgery in future. We left after picking up the medicines.

I was looking forward to the treat of ice cream and hot roasted salty whole peanuts and lentils. We sat inside the famous air conditioned ice cream parlour. My mother ordered full portion of ice cream i.e. two large dollops for me and milk shake for her. It was a sheer heavenly experience for me. I tucked into the ice cream nonstop. My mother kept looking at me and then said,

"Hey, take it easy. You will choke otherwise. There is no hurry; we will be taking a ride in a rickshaw up to the small bridge separating the village's dusty road."

I was excited at the prospect of having a ride in the rickshaw. That was a luxury for us.

"But, you will not mention a word about the ride to anyone in the house or in the village, understood?" She said that as she finished drinking the milkshake. I affirmed and licked the plate to finish the melted cream.

Little, partially dressed children who stood in the hot sun outside the entrance to the parlour were looking at me, licking the cream. I was too young to realise their plight. The proprietor kept swearing at them as he told them to go away. They didn't move. My mother noticed me looking at them. She drew my attention,

"Come on love, we will have to catch a rickshaw. It is getting late. Don't mention that we had these things here to anyone at home."

As we came out of the parlour, I could see still those children standing and starring at us.

My mother bought roasted peanuts and whole lentils, some for the people at home and some for us to eat on the way home. As the rickshaw made a slow meandering bumpy ride on the half tarmac and half dusty road leading towards the village, we were shaken and tossed up and down. Some of the peanuts and lentils fell on the floor of the rickshaw. My mother requested the driver to slow down the ride.

"Aunty, if I were to slow this, we will never make it to the small bridge. The engine will stop and to restart, it requires more fuel. I have a little fuel left for my return to the city." spoke the driver in a croaky voice, the result of chewing tobacco mixtures. His eyes were red. For a moment, I thought he was drunk. We clutched on to the side handles until we reached the bridge. My mother had paid the fares in advance. The driver asked mother if he could take us to our home. The mother refused his help and he drove away towards the city.

"Ba, I still get frightened of walking on this road. I have heard stories about monkeys jumping on us to get things from our hands. I also heard that there are robbers hiding in the bushes here". I looked around as I spoke.

"Now there are no robbers and the monkeys here. The village council has directed some folks to keep a regular watch here. We will be OK, my love". After a glance towards me, she quickly scanned the area. She could see a person sitting under a large tree, smoking BIDI, a hand rolled cigarette, and waving his arms at us.

"Hello Babubhai, how are you?" greeted my mother.

"Oh, I am fine. It is very scorching heat. Where have you been?" he said as he stood up.

"I went to see my doctor. I am not feeling well nowadays. How is your family?" she asked him as we stood near him.

"All are well. Here, let me carry all those things. I am about to return home anyway" he took couple of items from us.

"Did you see any robber today, uncle?" I asked. Babubhai smiled as he looked at me and said,

"No my son, there are no more robbers here. I tell you what, I saw that little boy who plays wonderful tunes on his flute. You know who I mean, don't you?"

"Raghav, the worker's son".

I wished I could play the flute. Soon, we arrived at home. Babubhai was invited for tea. My grandmother enquired generally about the trip and her daughter, my aunt in the city. She appeared very pleased to receive a packet of biscuits from her daughter. I felt very sad again to observe her happiness. Why couldn't she be so happy to see us? Why didn't she give money for the transport and snacks?

After a quick bath, I settled down for tea. My mother began to prepare the evening meals. She looked very tired but as no one in the house volunteered to prepare the meals, she being the eldest daughter-in-law had to work in the kitchen.

My father spent most of his life time in Africa. Whenever he visited the family, he didn't take us to the city or any other villages.'

Rahul's memories came to a sudden halt as Mum said,

"Here, drink this; it will do you good. Don't go outside today. The weather is bad. You can go to the TV room and watch something or rest on the sofa. I will get your dinner ready for later. I have cooked your favourite rice with vegetables in vine leaves, Greek style."

Rahul fell asleep in the living room for a long time. Mum had switched off the room light. When he awoke, it was night.

DIVORCE

A few months later on the estate, one night, when Rakhi was asleep in a bed next to Devi's bed, Dinesh entered the room and slowly approached towards Rakhi. As he reached near, he put his hand on her mouth and quickly saddled on top of her. Rakhi was startled, shocked and powerless. Dinesh whispered that if she made any noise he would kill her. Dinesh, being the person in the authority, would use force or power to humiliate, control, hurt or violate a woman. Rakhi couldn't say anything as Dinesh kept his hand very tightly on her mouth. He then tore off her blouse and began to suck a breast. She remained ineffective in her struggle to free herself. She wanted to scream but felt paralysed by fear. She tried to look in the direction of Devi but couldn't move her head. She stretched her arm towards Devi's bed but couldn't reach the bed as Dinesh was by now in the process of raping her. By now, she was frightened, numb and powerless. After a few minutes, he quickly left the room.

Rakhi's cry woke up Devi. Rakhi didn't say anything about the rape. She was trembling in the dark. She said that she had pain in her stomach. As Devi went to bring some herbal medicine for her, Rakhi sat on the edge of the bed feeling guilty, angry and ashamed. Previously, Rakhi trusted Meera and validated her feelings to recover from the shock. Now, she had no one to go to.

Rakhi couldn't tell anyone about the repeated rapes she endured in the subsequent year as no one would believe her. She was too frightened to write about this to Rahul. The rapes were depressing experiences that she couldn't shift out of her mind. So when she went to her father's place, she declared her intention of getting a divorce. Naturally, her father wanted to know the reasons for her decision. Rakhi didn't give the real reasons but simply said that she couldn't bear the burden of duties she had to perform. She pointed out that she had to wake up very early in the morning to milk the cows; to prepare breakfast for several people in the house and the workers; to see that by ten in the morning, she properly executed all the laundry work; then to prepare lunch and so on. Her day ended at midnight every day. She had hardly time for her food because of her involvement; and this affected her health.

Her father explained to her about her duties towards Rahul's family.

"It is your home and it is natural to find the work hard at first. You must go. How will I show my face to the people if you were to get divorced?"

Rakhi cried in front of Bhabhu but the latter could do nothing contrary to her father's instructions. Although Rakhi felt angry, she abandoned the divorce idea after much persuasion from Bhabhu who explained,

"Beti, we live in a society where the freedom to express all our personal feelings is not allowed. I understand that you are working hard; I can see that from your thin body. I am very concerned about you. Is there any other reason that makes you think of divorce?"

Rakhi felt a jolt as she heard Bhabhu's question. She quickly composed herself and said,

"There are no other reasons, Bhabhu. I am just tired of the work I have to perform in the house at the farm."

"Your grandparents are very understanding and you could speak to your Mani Ma at Pinsad about the work you have to do on the farm. I am sure she will do something about it for you."

"Do you realise how powerful Dinesh uncle is? He rules over everyone. No matter what the granddad say to him he always has his way. He gets very angry and everyone suffers. I don't think I should talk to Mani Ma. I will carry on with the work and try to be in Pinsad with Ma."

They gave her some money and said that if she needed more she should ask for it at anytime. She remembered what Ba had told her to avoid the rapes; that she must stay away from Dinesh. So, she decided to go to Pinsad. She persuaded Mani Ma to keep her with her.

"Beti, you can stay here as long as you like, but you should realise that whenever Dinesh needs someone to look after the children in the absence of Devi, you will have to go." Rakhi nodded in agreement but wasn't happy.

A few months later, she complained of pain in her stomach. She was given a herbal concoction to settle the pain. However, it didn't disappear and became a persistent complaint. Her health began to deteriorate as she couldn't eat well.

Dinesh got concerned about Rakhi getting pregnant; He said to Rakhi, "I think you should have a contraceptive fitted in case something untoward happened to you."

Rakhi irately refused to go through the procedure.

Then, Rakhi's pain became severe. When she went to her parent's, she told her Bhabhu about it. They went to see a specialist doctor in the nearby city of Bardoli. The diagnoses indicated that she had advanced growth of appendicitis, which needed surgery urgently—Rakhi was hospitalised. Her in-laws were informed.

JOURNEY TO THE WEST

Jogi was concerned about the events appertaining Rakhi's health. He was responsible for her well-being. When he heard about Rakhi's critical condition before the operation, he angrily told Mani,

"Didn't you realise how bad her abdominal pain was?"

"I had noticed it and had asked her if she wanted to visit the doctor but she refused. I don't think that she herself had realised the seriousness of the pain"

"Make sure that she remains in Sakri until she is well enough to walk about. Don't call her here early. I will tell Dinesh also to let her stay away and not call to the estate."

When Dinesh was informed of the event, he suspected that the operation could have been for an abortion. He got very concerned and visited Sakri to ascertain the truth. When Rakhi saw him in the house, she went upstairs in the bedroom and told Bhabhu not to allow him to see her. Dinesh was given the documents relating to the operation. He returned to the estate that evening.

Rahul was unaware of the events taking place in India. The grandfather wrote to Rahul to say that he was to send Rakhi to him. Dinesh became furious when he heard about this. He had a ferocious argument with his father. He said,

"Bapa, shouldn't you have informed me about your decision to send Rakhi to England? How is Rahul going to support her? He will have to find another place to live. That would mean more expenses. You know the conditions in Mozambique are bleak. It is almost impossible even to send £50 to him because of restrictions on money transfer."

Jogi remained silent for a few minutes. Then he said,

"You haven't realised how poor Rakhi's health has become lately. Suppose something untoward happened to her; what are you going to say to Rahul? We haven't disclosed to Rahul about her poor health. He probably assumes that all is well with her. No, I can't take the risk. She should go to Rahul as quick as possible."

Dinesh didn't argue further with his father and reluctantly decided to arrange all the formalities for her travel. He instructed the family travel agent that the preparation for travel documents should be prolonged as much as it could be. This was to buy time so he could continue raping Rakhi. However, he wasn't successful as his father insisted that she should stay with him as they were getting old and needed someone to look after them. Devi remained on the estate to manage the farm business for a long time. Meanwhile Dinesh couldn't go near Rakhi.

After one year, Dinesh obtained her passport and instructed his son, Suresh to fix a booking for a flight to London. They gave her few cheap saris, but no money, as a going away presents. She didn't speak English and was concerned about the journey. A person, from the nearby village, travelling to London, agreed to look after her.

Rakhi went to Sakri to bid farewell to all. As she stepped out of the car, she instantly cried as her father held her in his arms. He said,

"Come my Beti, let's go inside the house. Don't cry. You should be with Rahul now."

Bhabhu came hurriedly and grabbed Rakhi and said,

"Oh my dear daughter, come and sit with me on the swing. What will we do without you?" Bhabhu quickly wiped her tears and then with her handkerchief cleaned Rakhi's tears. She held her face and continued,

"Yes, you must go to Rahul. It has been a long time." A servant brought water for both. Rakhi looked at the servant and said,

"Pali, I will miss you. Who will comb my hair in England? Stay with Bhabhu as long as you can and help her."

"I am going to miss you too. Look after Jamai(Son-in-law) well and feed him good food. You too, eat well. Look after your health." Pali quickly turned around as she began to cry and walked towards the kitchen.

"I have got some saris and slippers for you. For my Jamai (Rahul), I have prepared a special sweetmeat that he likes." said Bhabhu pointing at a small bag containing the said items.

Champa came rushing in Rakhi's house as soon as she heard that Rakhi had come. She got hold of Rakhi and embraced her as she shed tears. She said,

"You lucky sister, finally you are to join your prince in London. Six years have been a long time. Your agony will now be over." Champa held her at a distance and smiled and said,

"Don't forget this friend of yours while you will be miles away entertaining your heart throb. I will be looking for your letters every month."

Rakhi with tears shook her head saying,

"Yes, yes. I will miss your company. Who will advise me in the time of my predicament? You have given me valuable help and advice in times of my difficulty." They both sat on the nearby bed. Champa enquired,

"What are your in-laws giving you to take with you to England?"

"They have given me few cheap saris and a pair of slippers." said Rakhi who then turned to Bhabhu and said,

"Bhabhu, I think I will take the usual kitchen items such as steel utensils and some basic spices. Rahul has got one pot for cooking vegetable curries. Although his aunts in Mozambique send condiments and pickles every two months by ship, they get moisturised from sea air. Oh, and some papadums and tea spices will come in handy."

At the time of Rakhi's return to Pinsad, many people of the village came to say good bye to her. Some presented flowers to her. It was late afternoon when Rakhi finally said good bye with tears to all. Bhabhu and Bhima said to her that they would join her on the day of departure from Pinsad.

For his lust to gain the absolute power, Dinesh diversified his energy towards becoming a popular person by generously giving financial assistance to various organisations. One of the biggest donations was made towards the building of a school in the local area. He became a popular person and soon got involved in politics. He began to live in a modern house in the nearby town where he could entertain ministers and lawyers. The children were sent off to a college in Ahmadabad, one of the big cities in Gujarat.

Rakhi had no idea about Rahul's latest appearance and wondered if she would recognise him at the airport. She asked her father to ask her brother, Chhotu in Dudley to accompany Rahul at the airport. Before boarding her flight, she wondered about the aeroplane, her seat, food, and other passengers. For her it was a strange experience. On boarding, she was escorted by a hostess, who spoke Hindi, to her seat and helped to fasten the seat belt. The take off was a frightening event for her. She closed her eyes until the aircraft had been in flight for a few minutes. The hostess asked her if she would like to have juice. She opened her eyes and shook her head indicating she didn't want it. The man who was to look after her during the flight said to her,

"I understand your nervousness. It is your first flight. Don't be frightened. Soon, you will be offered something to eat by the hostess."

Rakhi looked at the man momentarily and said,

"I don't want to eat anything. Please tell the woman not to wake me up." She rested her face on her right side of the seat and soon closed her eyes clutching her purse. She began to imagine about Rahul.

'What will he be like? Perhaps tall and handsome and maybe his skin colour will be fair by now. I hope Chhotu will be with him. They may have arranged for food for today. Bhabhu and Bapa must be heading for Navsari; they will get very tired and worried about me until Rahul informs them of my arrival. I wonder about England; people say that it is very cold there and has plenty of snow, just like cotton fluffs. I only have one jersey; I hope Rahul and Chhotu have something warm for me to wear; but then, how would they know what to bring for a woman?'

Rakhi was deep in sleep by now.

The man woke her up after several hours of flight when it was announced about filling some forms for customs and immigration. A hostess had given forms for Rakhi to the man. He explained to her what was required to declare to customs. Rakhi told him that she had one quilt only for her personal use. There was nothing else for anyone. She secured her passport and the air ticket from the man and turned her face away from him. He asked,

"Where does your husband live?"

She looked towards him and said,

"London".

"What is he doing?"

"He is studying".

"How long has he been in London?"

"Six years".

He smiled and said,

"Well, at last, both of you will be together after all those years. I wish you a long and happy life."

She smiled in appreciation of his good wishes and turned her face away.

Rahul and Chhotu came to London airport nearly two hours before the arrival time of Rakhi's flight. However, the flight was delayed further by an hour. They had drinks in the bar. Rahul didn't take alcoholic drinks. Chhotu had a pint of lager. Rahul settled for a half pint of lemonade. Chhotu said,

"Rahul Patel, since you are going to see my sister after six years, have you any idea how she looks now?"

"No, tell me Mr Patel"

"Well, she has changed a lot since you got married. Now she is slightly taller and thin. She is fully trained in the house work. She cooks food which is finger licking good. She has been a hard working woman in your house."

"Wow that is wonderful news. You said she is thin. Why?"

"She had to learn a lot about domestic work in Pinsad. It was very hard for her in the beginning to work for long hours. But, she soon picked up the craft and become very popular with your Mani Ma and Dada."

Rahul knew about her hard work already from her letters and concluded that she ate very little.

An announcement was made of the arrival of her flight. Rahul and Chhotu stood by the arrival entrance stretching their necks to see Rakhi coming out. Behind several passengers, Rakhi walked slowly towards the exit door searching for Rahul and Chhotu. She spotted them on the left hand side of the walk-way. She was accompanied by the man who looked after her in the plane. Suddenly, Chhotu shouted enthusiastically,

"Ben (sister), we are here".

Rakhi gave a smile and introduced the man. He soon left them. Rakhi glanced shyly towards Rahul for a brief moment and turned to Chhotu,

"How are you and Bhabhi (Chhotu's wife)?"

"We are well, how are Bapa and Bhabhu?"

"They are OK. They pass their regards to you. They said that you should write to them regularly."

Then, Rakhi turned bashfully towards Rahul,

"How are you?"

Rahul looked up and spoke to God,

"Oh my Master, put your hand over my heart lest it stops thumping on seeing her".

Rahul quickly went to her and held her by her shoulders and looked straight into her eyes. Chhotu turned his face away as Rahul kissed Rakhi who felt as if she was going to melt away. She softly said,

"People are watching us. I am embarrassed." Her face turned pink. She looked down. Rahul hugged her and escorted her towards the exit door. Chhotu went ahead to bring the car near the door.

"How are you my goddess? You look very thin. Did Ma not let you have enough food?" They walked slowly outside the door and waited for the car.

"Ma wouldn't do that to me. She is so kind. Both Dada and Ma miss you very much." Rakhi tried to come off his hand clutch. Rahul wouldn't let her go, he said,

"I know people in India don't do it like this. Here it is normal. From now onward, we will be walking hand in hand in our new life"

Rakhi wore the same white sari she had worn when she got married. She was delighted to see her brother and Rahul. However, she was shocked to see the pigmented face of Rahul. She assumed that he had some form of disease. As they drove towards the house, she queried:

"What happened to your face? You never mentioned about it in your letters."

"It is just a change in the facial skin colour. It isn't infectious. The specialist told me that it will go away in the future."

"Oh!" Rakhi was unhappy. Rahul realised that and keeping his face on the road, said softly,

"As we have not consummated our marriage, you are free to go separately. There is nothing to lose, is there?" Rahul then looked at her for a couple of seconds.

She deliberated; she thought of all those years she endured cruel events in India. She had shown devoted fidelity towards Rahul. She considered his remark very inapt. She asked,

"If the situation was reversed, what would you have done?"

"I wouldn't survive without you" He said with smile. Rakhi blushed; as she glanced at her brother, Chhotu said,

"See, my sister is not so illiterate, is she?" He shook Rahul's shoulders from behind.

"OK, I now see what I have to put up with", he said looking at Rakhi's happy face.

They arrived at the bungalow in Twickenham. Rahul and his three close friends had rented it. It had three bedrooms and a small kitchen with an adjoining large conservatory. The garden at the back of the house was reasonably large. There was a garage on the side of the house.

The winter was approaching. Rakhi settled down happily. During the day, Rahul attended a college. When he returned home, Rakhi would complain about her boredom,

"I try to see the programmes on television during the day but I don't understand a word of what they say. I get a headache".

"Sorry my darling, but you have to put up with this situation. I tell you what; I will give you a book of the alphabet to study daily. In the evening we both will go through the letters and other things. Is that OK?"

"Do I have to study English at this age?" She looked at Rahul like an innocent child would. Rahul made her sit on a sofa. He held her shoulders and said,

"You are never too old to learn anything in this world, my dear. When I came here in 1955, I didn't know about writing, reading and speaking the English language. You are lucky that I am here to help you. I was frustrated when I began to learn the language. I joined a secretarial collage in central London for the initial study of subjects required to pass an ordinary level examination. Very often, I sat in the classes just looking at the teachers talking. I wondered if I would ever achieve my objectives in this country. I missed you and the family; the food, the house and the society, the village and farms etc. etc. But, I had to force myself to learn the English language without which I couldn't have been able to study other subjects like history, geography, physics and chemistry. I tell you it was a very depressing life.

However, for the fear of going back to Mozambique and not being able to study further there but to join the family business, I decided, my dear, to study here for a degree in Economics. You have to learn English and I will assist you in every way I can. While I am at college, soon after the house work is done, you try to read and write English."

As Rahul kissed her lips, she smiled a little and hugged him. Rahul could feel her body trembling. Rakhi remembered the first kiss he gave her at night in the flat in Bombay.

In November, Rahul and Rakhi decided to celebrate Diwali festival with friends by having the first pakka Gujarati food, prepared by Rakhi. Some thirty people were invited. Both began the preparation of variety of food the night before. Rakhi decided to prepare pilau rice, two types of vegetable curries, mainly of aubergines and potatoes and French beans with petite pois. Also, she fried PURIS (a small round chapatti look) and small VADAS (Pakodas made of semolina with crushed lentils and yoghurt) and various other sweet and spicy tit-bits. In addition to rice pudding with ground nutmeg, she prepared yoghurt curry to go with the pilau rice. Rahul helped her by washing up pots and pans and tasting of various items. Having had the taste of various things, he looked at Rakhi and said,

"Hey, I must salute you Rakhi for preparing excellent food items. How on earth did you learn cooking so well?"

"I learnt it the hard way. Most of the things I learnt from Ba. The grandma also taught a few traditional things like making of Sev (Spaghetti) and sweetmeats for special occasions.

"What you mean the hard way?"

"Both would taste everything I cooked and if it was not up to standard, they insisted that I start all over again. Bless their souls, they meant well but I was crying sometimes." Rakhi stopped frying an item and looked at Rahul with a serious face. Rahul held her face and pulled her close and said,

"How lucky am I to have a wonderful wife like you. I am sorry that you had to learn the hard way but it will pay, don't you agree?" As he kissed her she said,

"Yes, now shall we get on with the work? It is going to be eleven o'clock and I feel tired and sleepy."

They woke up early to finish off the cooking and tidy up the lounge where all the guests would be sitting on the floor. There was no larger place to accommodate them with tables and chairs. They had invited thirty friends. The evening weather turned out to be cold with hazy sunlight. Before the guests began to arrive, Rahul played Hindi film songs on the tape recorder for background music. He wore a light blue shirt with dark blue tie and darker blue trousers. Rakhi wore a beautiful embroidered light blue silk sari, given to her by her friend Champa, and, her favourite jasmine perfume.

Every guest greeted Rakhi and Rahul with Namaste (I bow to God within you). Rahul introduced Rakhi to each person. Lot of the guests presented flowers and small gifts to Rakhi. After the arrival of all guests, the ladies gathered to offer help to Rakhi. Some praised Rakhi's beautiful looks. Others who tried to converse in English to Rakhi soon realised the embarrassment they were causing her and apologised to her in Gujarati by saying 'MAF KARJO BHABHI'(Forgive us, sister-in-law). To them, Rakhi was older and therefore was referred as Bhabhi.

Soon beers and wines and soft drinks were put in circulation. Some commented on the lovely music. Everyone was cordial to the hosts. The ladies went in the kitchen and began to give help in putting the food items in separate large bowls and plates and deliver to the central area of the floor of the lounge.

"Bhabhi, the aroma of the food is lovely. We are very hungry now. We never had such Gujarati food since we have been in this country." Some complimented.

"Thank you all, but please try the food first and then tell me about it." Rakhi replied with a smile. For the first time, she began to notice the appreciation she was having from totally unknown people. She felt really good after a long time in her life. All sat in a circular form around the food items. Some ladies began to serve the food. Rahul and Rakhi joined the guests. Those who began to eat came out with full praise for the various items. Some went sentimental about the items they rarely had in their life and that it had reminded them of their homes.

"Bhabhi, Dhanyavad (congratulation) for the fantastic food. Some of these ladies could learn about cooking from you."

"Yes, bhabhi, we will be honoured" said the ladies.

"Thank you all. You are all welcome to learn from me." Rakhi responded with enthusiasm.

They spent almost an hour eating the food. No one could get up as they had far more food than usual. Rahul and Rakhi were very happy to provide the opportunity to all to have Gujarati food. As night fell, the guests began to leave offering their many thanks to Rakhi and Rahul.

DISASTERS: BOTH FINANCIAL AND HEALTH WISE

Just as Rahul and Rakhi were settling down in their new life, disturbing news came from the uncles in Mozambique. They would no longer be able to send money due to the political upheaval in their part of the country. The new authority decided that all the citizens of India must leave the country. At the same time, the Government authorities put all the Indian citizens in an enclosed area without allowing the retention of their possessions. The authorities maintained that it was for the safety of the Indians. Eventually, many Indians were sent to India by ship. Some went to Brazil, South America.

Rahul mentioned to his close friends about his financial hardship. He couldn't take up any employment as a foreign student in the country. One friend helped him financially for a short period. A close friend knew someone who could get the information regarding Rahul's residential status. Rahul's father, Govind, worked in Africa. The British authority in India issued an Anglo-Indian passport to his father. Rahul submitted that passport with relevant application forms for naturalisation as a British subject. Rahul had spent more than five years and had not become a burden to the society here. He provided appropriate reference letters. His application was successful. His friend, a civil servant, found a job for him in his office. He was given a clerical post dealing with servicing of credit insurance for exported goods from the UK to buyers abroad. After a few years, Rahul became a permanently established civil servant.

THE GOOD NEWS

Both, Rahul and Rakhi were strolling about gently in the back garden of their house. Then suddenly Rahul looked at Rakhi and said,

"If I could reach the sky, I would bring the stars to spread at your feet". Rahul was in a romantic mood. He had his right arm over Rakhi's shoulder.

A moment later,

"If I could reach the sky, I would bring the moonlight to spread on a road for you to come to me. We would steal the happiness and enjoy it there". Rakhi was equally in a good mood. She had her left arm over Rahul's shoulder. Rahul saw the ocean of love in her eyes.

Suddenly, she remembered an inferiority complex she had for not being able to learn further than the 7th standard level due to her circumstances in India. One had to pass twelve standards of education to get admission into a college. She had noticed that Rahul also felt the same way about his education.

"Why do you tell people that you didn't finish your degree? Why lower your credibility when you had reached the final year of the BSc Economics degree?" Rakhi asked.

Rahul was elated and said,

"Yes darling, you are absolutely right. I say that only to a person who is more intelligent than I am. I feel sad knowing that I don't have that person's ability. You see my darling, I feel hurt when I find myself in that situation."

"Well, don't underestimate your intelligence. I think you are clever," she said with a lovely smile. They moved forward slowly towards the kitchen door. Then they stopped and Rahul said,

"Remember that picture of us that reflects our closeness and smiles? I feel like that right now."

Rakhi hugged him and said,

"I have good news for you, dear" She looked at Rahul.

"What?" Rahul became curious. He looked in her sparkling eyes.

"I am expecting."

Rahul held her tightly for a moment. He realised then why she was so cheerful and had worn a beautiful sari that had patterns of light blue flowers and faint yellow leaves. He kissed her and said,

"Thank you. Hey, that's good news. I love you, you almighty Amba (The mother Earth)." He turned her round and round until he realised that she started to wobble. He stopped and said,

"Are you OK my darling?"

"A little bit dizzy but I am alright now. Let's go inside the house. I have to make some telephone calls."

She disclosed the news to her brother and to many relatives. She was experienced in how a woman should prepare herself for her baby. Rahul had no clue about it. An aunt called Nani had two children of her own. She supported Rakhi during the pregnancy by staying with her.

They named the newly born child Prakash. It meant 'light'. He was truly divine light in their lives. He was born in the local hospital. They went through a great hardship to survive without the financial help from home and Africa. Rahul managed to earn a decent income. He paid more than half of his income towards the mortgage he incurred. Before the birth of Prakash, a college friend furnished details of the London County Council's scheme of one hundred percent loan for a house purchase by young couple like Rahul and Rakhi. Their application for house loan was successful. They bought a two bed room terraced house in the Brentford area. The LCC granted the purchase price less one hundred pounds that Rahul had to pay upfront.

After buying the house, they accommodated a cousin named Naran, who came from Africa. His father was very poor but had hoped that the son would study further and have a better future. The father couldn't support him financially. Rahul had instructions from the uncles in Mozambique to support Naran. However, this made Rahul's life very difficult when the uncles and Naran's father had to evacuate the country.

Rahul undertook additional work with the directory enquiry office. He would have a quick meal after his day job and begin the other job in the evening until eleven at night. During the weekends, both Rahul and Naran decided to sell Indian groceries and vegetables to various clients, residing in the south and the northwest corners of London. They bought a second hand van for this business.

Naran got married to a girl named Nalini. She was born in London to parents who ran a wholesale business of Indian vegetables and groceries. Rakhi thought that by having Nalini in the family, life would be little less hectic. No such luck came her way. Nalini was lazy and did very little work in the house. She wasn't interested in learning and cooking of Indian food. Her favourite food was chips, crisps and readymade meals. Most of the time, she read books of romance sitting inside the cupboard eating chips. Naran was aware of this but could do nothing. Once he said to her,

"I have noticed that you are always in this room when Bhabhi (Rakhi) is busy cooking downstairs. She prepares a variety of tasty food. Why don't you take advantage of her know-how and learn cooking too?"

"I don't want to know about variety of food. I don't like some food" Nalini said.

"All you seem to know is frying chips, boiling potatoes and cook readymade meals. I wish you'd learn about something new from Bhabhi" Naran suggested.

"Since we are going to stay here, you should be OK regarding food. I can make my own meals." she said.

Naran disliked Nalini's strange habits. She didn't join the family gathering in the evenings. Both argued loudly. Rakhi often heard loud noises coming from their bedroom late at night. The more arguments they had, the more determined Nalini became not to do anything. Naran was disappointed about Nalini's obstinate nature. He asked for Rahul's advice,

"Rahul, I don't understand her behaviour. What should I do? I am getting less sleep at night and feel very tired during the daytime. It affects my work."

"I reckon that she wasn't taught about cooking of various foods. Or, it could be that she wasn't interested in cooking. She may like to live independently. Why don't you move out to a different location and make a new start in your life?" Rahul advised. Naran agreed to move. The business was wound up and Naran and Nalini left the house to settle in north London. Rahul and Rakhi were sad to see them go. They had no money. Rahul wondered what they would do in North London. Before they left, Rahul said to Naran,

"We will miss you both. Let me know if we could be of any help to you." He could detect tears in Naran's eyes.

One bright sunny day, when Rakhi was coming downstairs to prepare a meal for lunch, she caught her sari underneath her foot and tumbled down the fourteen steps. On landing at the bottom of the stairs her body somersaulted and she received a knock on her lower back from the wall. Everything appeared normal to them and thought nothing further of the incidence. Six months later, one morning Rakhi cried and said she couldn't move her both legs. Rahul could see problems arising if Rakhi's situation was very serious. He thought of Prakash's welfare.

The GP examined her at home and suggested that she should be taken to the local hospital immediately by an ambulance. After investigation, a consultant said that her coccyx was damaged. This was the tragedy that was to bother both for many years to come. Rakhi was put on painkillers and became somewhat disabled at times. In the initial months, her pain subsided for a while due to the medication. She envisaged her total disability in the years to come. The doctors said that Rakhi would suffer increasing pain as the years go by.

After several months of double work schedules, lack of general rest, intake of imbalanced food and anxiety, Rahul contracted TB. His symptoms were tiredness, loss of weight, fainting and shortness of breath. One morning as he was resting on a chair in a friend's house, he collapsed. He was taken to the hospital in Isleworth area by ambulance. After examination of his condition, a consultant looked at him and said,

"Mr. Rahul Patel, you have an advanced condition of tuberculosis of lungs. Your right lung appears to be more affected. Now please listen very carefully. I am confident of curing you provided I get your full support in every respect. Do you follow me?"

Rahul, aged thirty looked in the consultant's eyes for a while. He could feel that GOD was present in front of him. How else can God help someone? A thought flashed by in his mind. He spoke with difficulty due to poor breathing,

"Sir, I surrender my life into your hands. I will do all that you wish me to do." Rahul started coughing. He was put on the bed. Rakhi was in tears. The consultant said to her,

"Don't worry my dear. He will be on his feet very soon." The Indian nurse who had accompanied the consultant translated what the doctor said to Rakhi. The latter sat on a chair next to Rahul's bed and stroked Rahul's head. In India, a person who had TB wasn't expected to survive. It was a certain death. Rakhi was horrified at the knowledge that Rahul could die also. Many friends and relatives consoled Rakhi. They said that with effective treatments of TB, patients got well and led a normal life for long time. As Rahul closed his eyes and fell asleep, she left the hospital.

Rahul's progress was quick after the administration of medication. His weight increased with the ever-increasing food intake. He was sent home at the end of the third month. Rakhi and Prakash were very happy to see him well. They were amused at the amount of food that Rahul had. He ate one whole honey melon after a substantial meal at lunch time. In the evening, he would have another melon after dinner. After a month, Rakhi got worried about Rahul eating large quantity of food. Rahul raised this issue with the GP who informed him that it was nothing to worry about. After sometime, Rahul began to eat less. He resumed his work after six months. He borrowed money to meet the expenses.

The family members in India knew about Rahul's health and financial difficulty. Manu had informed them. Dinesh was keen to see Rahul, Rakhi, and Prakash back in India. Rahul didn't like the idea but he had no choice. He agreed to go. However, before departing, he reluctantly handed the responsibility of selling the house and dealings of any other matters to his brother-in-law, Manu. In addition, he secured the consent of his department, for his reinstatement in the post he held, should he have to return to England.

MORE TROUBLES AT BOMBAY AIRPORT

May was the hottest month of the year 1970. Rahul, Rakhi, and Prakash returned to India permanently. They carried as many possessions as they could, including all the cine films that Rahul had made of holidays and family events. Little did they realise that the films were going to be a big problem in the Bombay customs. It was an age of pornographic materials, illegally produced and smuggled through the customs internationally. The business, being a hot cake, gave very high returns to the dealers. Rahul and Rakhi were having argument over a bag full of soft drinks. They had left them in the aircraft as the stress of leaving England permanently far outweighed anything else. Their excess baggage went to a cargo shed. In the customs hall, several officers, having noticed the quantity of films in the baggage, suspected that the family was smuggling pornographic materials. Thus, the targeted check of every piece of luggage meant that Rahul and Rakhi, were grilled for hours in the custom area. Some of the officers persistently cross-examined their stories. Both of them told the truth; that the films were of family records such as weddings, birthdays, and holidays. Prakash was seven years old and remained with Rakhi all the time.

Having realised that the officers were not satisfied with the statements so far, Rahul suggested if the officers would like to see samples of the films. To his surprise, they agreed. Rahul set up the projector that he had brought. About three officers selected several film reels. The contents of the first reel were wedding scenes; the show went on for a half an hour. The officers told Rahul to continue with the showing of other reels. After about another hour of showing of several reels, one of the officers went away into a room nearby. Several other officers in the hall gathered to see the films projected on a white wall. They went on making comments, whenever they could recognise places in London and other cities.

The officer who had gone into the room came out and escorted Rahul to that room. He saw a man in plain clothes sitting on a chair in front of a large desk. He remained seated as he said,

"I am a senior officer. Please take a seat."

Rahul sat on a chair rather nervously. He had heard about the harassments caused by the officers in Bombay customs. He wasn't sure of what the next event was to be. The officer continued writing something on paper for a while. Then, he asked Rahul to come to his side and open one of the drawers of the desk. As Rahul opened the middle drawer, he saw several reels of films inside.

"Yes, you see Mr Patel, we get lots of pornographic films smuggled everyday here. Since you have many films in your baggage, we had no option but to examine the contents of your films. Please accept my apology for the inconvenience caused to you and your family. Incidentally, your wife and son are outside the hall. You may go out, thank you."

Rahul took a deep breath and managed to hide his anger at the whole incident. He appreciated the civilised manner of the senior officer. The other officers in the hall weren't so nice. They laughed and made jokes about pornographic films. One officer commented to his fellow officer that even some families were involved in importation of prohibited materials. Rahul walked out and collected his baggage, ensuring that the films that were out on the bench were the same in number that he counted when projecting. The officers, who saw him struggling to pack the reels in the bags, didn't help. Customs officers generally don't help passengers to pack baggage.

Rakhi and Prakash were relieved to see Rahul coming out of the customs hall after two hours. Until then, no one had told them what was happening. Rakhi was crying. Rahul consoled her and explained to her about the reason for the delay. Amrit, Rahul's cousin, had come to receive them from Pinsad where Rahul and others were going to stay.

They took a taxi to the cargo area of the airport to collect the unaccompanied baggage. After another two hours wait in the scorching sun, they managed to clear and collect the bags. The taxi took them to the central railway station for the onward journey by train to the village.

Amrit purchased the tickets and hired a coolie to pick up the luggage. As they approached a compartment of the train, a group of plain-clothes people rushed towards Rahul and pushed him in the compartment. Amrit had realised that something was wrong and quickly escorted Rakhi and Prakash to another compartment; He told the coolie to put the luggage in the compartment. He then requested Rakhi and Prakash to remain calm and say nothing to anyone. He, then, went near to the compartment where Rahul was detained to see what was happening. He saw Rahul held against the wall of the compartment by a burly man who appeared to be examining Rahul's coat pockets. Another person was looking into the briefcase, taking things out and throwing on the floor. Amrit heard the burly man asking Rahul,

"Where did you get this money?"

"It is the money I earned in England. I am coming home permanently," said a very frightened, exhausted, and disheartened Rahul. He almost cried at this unexpected incident. The incident that occurred just before leaving London flashed before his eyes.

One late evening in May, Rahul and Rakhi, were driving home after a farewell visit to a close friend. Suddenly, a cat began to cross the road unexpectedly. Rahul couldn't stop the car. The cat's head sheared off and flew towards the right side of the road. Rakhi was terrified. Rahul continued driving the car. Rakhi said,

"This is a bad omen, very bad omen. What is happening to us? I hope nothing will happen to us in India." She appeared very distressed. Rakhi held traditional views about life in general. If someone died or crossed a path which one took on a good mission, it was considered a bad omen.

"Don't worry my dear. This sort of orthodox belief can't be true," uttered Rahul.

As he remembered this incident, he feared if the orthodox view could be true.

The burly, dark brown man who had held him released his grip on him. He then produced his I.D. card showing that he was from the customs investigation department. He and his staff left the compartment. Rahul sat on the bench and began to sort out his things that were all over the place. Other passengers, mainly women, were saying kind things to Rahul and helped to pick up items. Amrit entered the compartment as soon as the customs people left. He secured things and helped Rahul to leave the section, designated specially for women passengers only.

Shaken and disheartened Rahul could hardly believe that all this was happening to him. Once again, Rakhi was in tears as she met Rahul. Amrit remained silent for a while. He offered water to Rahul and the others. Rahul looked in the wet eyes of Rakhi and said,

"Darling, you were right after all. That bloody cat has done all this to us. Wish we could take a plane back to England." He wiped Rakhi's tears.

As the train pulled out laboriously from the platform, they felt the somewhat cooler breeze. Amrit kept an eye on the luggage. The others slept. It was a slow creeping 'local' train journey to the village.

It was hot in late evening when they arrived in Pinsad. They were greeted by Jogi and Mani. Rahul bent down to Jogi's and Mani's feet. Rakhi followed the procedure. Rahul hugged Jogi who said,

"Welcome Beta (Son), I am so glad to see you all." Prakash was lifted by Mani who said,

"How are you my third generation's first prince? You look very tired. Let's get inside the house."

They entered the house to be greeted by other members of the family. After they refreshed and had little food they were shown the bedrooms upstairs. There were no fans. Windows were covered with mesh wires to stop mosquitoes entering the room. Rakhi complained about severe pain in her back. She was exhausted from the journey. She couldn't sit on a chair due to pain in her damaged coccyx. She fell asleep on a bed. Rahul put Prakash who was half asleep on to another bed. Rahul was feeling tired too but went downstairs to say good night to others. Apart from Jogi and Mani no one seemed happy to see Rahul family. The cousins, now grown up, left late at night for the estate as they had to attend the school.

After few days, they found out that the female members of the household were making their life very difficult by creating impossible situations for them to overcome. Due to her disabling spinal injury, Rakhi was confined to bed. When it came to secure admission for Prakash in an English medium school in Navsari, they needed a significant sum of money as a donation. Rahul thought that the family would pay the money but that didn't happen. Instead, the family chose another school which Prakash didn't like. He found the students were way behind in certain subjects. Even the teachers spoke poor and sometimes incorrect English.

Rakhi cried because Prakash was very unhappy about his residency and the school. Dinesh's sister, who lived near the school, agreed to accommodate Prakash in her house. Having been brought up in England, Prakash couldn't adjust to different idiosyncrasies typical of local people and general life. He hardly understood the language of boys in the school. Rahul was aware of all these things but felt helpless against the dictatorial orders of Dinesh.

Dinesh had planned for Rahul to go into business with his son Suresh. Dinesh introduced them to various business people, hoping Rahul would agree to work for a business. Rahul realised that he had to find some work in order to support his family. His grandfather helped him with limited money without the knowledge of Dinesh. The potential business offers were not those in which Rahul had any experience. He tried to buy time until he discovered a business of manufacturing textile that he could take an interest in. However, he didn't like the idea of going into the business with Suresh because he suspected that Suresh would do a supervisory job while he would do the hard work. In addition, knowing the possessive and dictatorial nature of Dinesh, he would end up with very little money in his hand.

Once, Rahul met a consultant for Rakhi's back pain in a nearby city. They stayed in a hostel for the treatment. At first Dinesh and his accomplices told Rahul that Rakhi's pain was purely psychological. In India, bribery works wonders. Dinesh wanted to prove that Rakhi was a fraud. Of course, the real reason was his unsuccessful attempts to rape her. Rahul was at a loss to realise why the others were trying to create difficulties for him. He was unaware still of the rapes that Rakhi had sustained before. Dinesh was hopeful of approaching Rakhi but he never got near her. He was frightened of Rahul believing that Rakhi must have told him about the rapes. Dinesh began to dislike Rahul and Rakhi. He created various situations to make them suffer.

The women of the house weren't interested in Rakhi's well being; on the contrary, they also began to believe that there was nothing wrong with her and actively created work situations for her. They knew that such work she wouldn't be able to carry out. Moreover, if they decided to go out in the evening to see a film or a drama show, they ensured that Rahul and Rakhi shuttled from one village to another. For this, they had to use public transport, even though the family had a car. The state run buses were very old and uncomfortable; the roads were bad; had many holes and uneven surfaces. It was unbearable for Rakhi. However, they had no choice. They took several buses to reach Pinsad. It became apparent to Rahul and Rakhi that they weren't welcomed in the house.

Jogi asked them, after they came through the front gate,

"Why have you come here in this unbearable heat?"

They both bowed down to touch Jogi's feet and slowly stood up. Rahul said,

"Dada, Dinesh uncle sent us here as they all were going somewhere."

"Didn't anyone tell you that they were going to see a film or something in Valsad?"

"No"

"Dinesh should have known that Rakhi has a lot of pain and it is the middle of hot summer. He is a fool to send you by bus when there is a car. Never mind, go inside and freshen up. Rakhi, you can rest in the room upstairs."

Mani Ma heard the conversation and after the couple went inside the house, she said to Jogi,

"Dinesh said that Rakhi was making it up about her pain. That she was a liar"

Jogi looked into her eyes and annoyingly said to Amba,

"Are you blind? Can't you see that she really suffers from pain? Why would she lie?"

Amba didn't answer and went inside the house.

Some days later, when Jogi was reading the newspaper, other members of the family gathered in the lounge. Amba remarked,

"People in the village are saying that Rahul is spending most of his time with Rakhi upstairs. It is damaging to our family reputation."

Jogi lifted his eyes slowly and looked at Amba for a few seconds. Then, he told her to call Rahul downstairs. Rana's wife went near the staircase and shouted for Rahul.

Upon his arrival downstairs, Rahul was told by Amba about the people's views. He slowly went near the bench where Jogi sat and took his place on the bench. He then scanned his eyes to see who was present inside the room and outside on the swing. It was late morning. The sunlight was brightly bathing the room. It was getting hot inside. Rahul spoke rather angrily,

"Is it not your responsibility to look after your own daughter-in-law then? If none of you are going to undertake the responsibilities then I have to take care of her, isn't it so? One of you must have publicised what goes on in this house. Did you not discredit the reputation of this family then?"

Rahul turned to Jogi and said,

"We have decided to leave India for England. We can't take anymore contrived ideas from anyone in this house. There has been a conspiracy, one after another, ever since we came here. We came for your help with our health and other problems, leaving behind all our things acquired with great difficulty in England. You wouldn't think even to give financial help to us. How do you think we survived here so far without money? Rakhi's parents are dead. You all should be responsible for her welfare. She should be accepted as the daughter of this house. What makes you think that she is a fraud? When we took Rakhi to see the doctor for her pain, Dinesh uncle had informed the consultant prior to Rakhi being seen suggesting that she was a fraud and her pain was simply psychological. I know this for a fact; a cousin who was with Dinesh uncle in the consultant's office told me. So please look at the reality in this family. If no one is to care for Rakhi, and should something serious happen to her, people will say to me and to all in this family that we neglected her. What about the credibility issue of this family then?" Rahul turned around and faced Jogi who intently heard what was said by Rahul.

"Go my son and be happy there. These people will not let you live in peace here. For some reason, Dinesh doesn't want you to live in India. I don't understand him. What are you going to do about your air tickets? No one will buy them here. In fact, Dinesh has instructed Manu in England, not to arrange for your tickets," said the grandfather. Dinesh did his best to create more difficulty for Rahul.

"I don't have to worry about the tickets, Dada. My good English friend will be glad to arrange for them" Rahul assured him.

"You go back and when you reach England send me a telegram confirming your safe arrival. I will send you my own one lakh rupees (Approximately £1335) for your use. I am sure your uncles and aunts aren't going to help you to settle here. You all have my blessings and ensure that you take good care of Rakhi and Prakash." Grandfather's voice mellowed as he spoke. A person, who heard what Jogi said, spoke from outside the front door,

"You are right Jogi, all will be better off in England. I wish them the best of luck. God bless Rakhi."

One morning Rahul, Rakhi, Prakash, and Suresh took the 'Flying Queen' train for Bombay. A non-resident visitor to India required a clearance certificate from the main tax office, when the stay exceeded by six months. Suresh took them to a family agent. He introduced Rahul and others as the members of Govind family. As the manager saw Rahul, he hastily moved forward towards Rahul and embraced him saying:

"So you are the son of Govindji; I am so delighted to meet you, Rahul. You look exactly like your father. He was a very good and honest man. I often think of him and now seeing you is like meeting him. Come and sit down here." They sat on the nearby chairs. He ordered cold drinks for them all. He enquired further,

"Rahul, tell me what can I do for you? Have you been here long?"

"I am so delighted to meet you, Sulemanji. We have been here for almost seven months and now we want to go back to England." Rahul stated.

"Why so soon? Is it our heat here?"

"Yes, the heat is unbearably stifling in this country. In any case, our presence can cause more problems for the family members as they have work to do. We saw what we had to and decided to return to England now."

The cold drinks arrived. All gulped the 'Thumbs Up' drink, dark blackberry coloured that tasted like a mixture of tinctured iodine and normal coca cola.

"Tell me, what can I do for you? When would you like to return to England?"

"Can you send us today?" Rahul said jokingly.

"Before you leave this country you will have to have clearance certificates from the tax office. I could send you today if you so wish."

"Come on Sulemanji, you can't do that today. For one thing, it takes two or three days to get those certificates, doesn't it?" Suresh enquired.

Sulemanji called his son, Rehman and confirmed that he could secure certificates on that day. He added further,

"The least I could do for the sake of my best friend, Govindji, and Rahul, is to pay a little sum of money to the right person in the tax office to get the approval stamps on the certificates".

Suresh was surprised to hear that.

"Thank you Sulemanji. We have to go back to the village after doing some last minute shopping here. There is no question of catching a flight tonight. However, I would appreciate if you can book us on a flight in a week's time. I will be requesting a friend in London to arrange for our single tickets to London. He will pay to Air India in London. Can you then issue the tickets here?" Rahul said.

Sulemanji confirmed that AIR INDIA office here would issue the tickets upon receiving the instructions from its London office. Suresh was surprised further at the decision made by Rahul without consulting his father.

After the shopping, they returned to the grandfather's village and disclosed the fact that Rahul's family would be leaving for England in a week's time. When Dinesh heard of this, he became angry but said nothing at first. When he arrived in Pinsad, he made a comment to the effect that modern people don't like consulting the elders. Like the people in the Western countries, they learn to adopt selfishness and disregard for their parents. Rahul, Rakhi, and Prakash took the grandfather's blessings and left for England.

TO ENGLAND AND
MORE TROUBLES

No one in the family gave any money to Rahul and the others. Everyone knew that Manu had put up the house in London for sale. The handling agent was on the verge of passing the house to a buyer when Rahul intervened. He put a stop to the sale much against the wish of Manu. Rahul's family entered the house to see that everything inside had gone. There was no furniture, beds, utensils etc. It was November and it was cold in the evenings. Luckily, the gas and electricity supplies were available. The three sat in front of the living room's gas fire. Rahul and Rakhi discussed the finance for food, beds, and bills. The outstanding mortgage had to be paid. They decided to borrow some money on a credit card immediately to provide food for Prakash and his school uniform. He joined the nearby school he'd attended before. Rahul got in touch with the staff section of the department he'd worked for. He was happy to hear that he could start work immediately. At the end of December, he got his first pay of £40 in his hand. Rahul, Rakhi, and Prakash began their new life in England.

After few years, another tragedy struck Rahul's family. A letter from Dinesh instructed Rahul to receive his son, Anil arriving from Canada. Anil was a student and got involved in serious trouble with the immigration authority in Canada. Soon Anil arrived in England before Rahul had his say. Rahul had to put him up initially. Anil joined a school to register himself as a foreign student. Rahul's expenses increased. Dinesh argued that the money sent to Rahul hitherto should be sufficient to support additional expenses of keeping Anil. Rahul informed Dinesh that the money that came from Africa had run out and there were hardly any savings left after the recent trip to India. Furthermore, he informed him that Anil was thinking of opening a grocery shop. Anil proposed that the present house was to be sold to raise the finance for the shop. Rahul made it clear that he wasn't going to sell the house. This created a conflict between Rahul and Anil.

"You are crazy to suggest that I sell this house to finance the purchase of a shop. Have you got any experience of running a shop? What sort of shop you want to buy? Sorry, I am not prepared to sell this house. What will happen if your business venture fails? We have been through many difficult circumstances and I can't take further risk." said Rahul.

"So you are going against my wish and have doubts about my ability to run a shop. What do you think my father will do to you?" said Anil.

"Whatever he might do, I am not frightened of him anymore. As to your ability to run a shop, I definitely think that you have no experience of a commercial undertaking. I am not prepared to sell this house." said Rahul. Anil made no further comment.

Dinesh secretly financed the project; he sent money through a third party. Anil created tension in the house by finding slightest excuses to cause furious arguments between Rakhi, Prakash, and Rahul. One late afternoon, he entered Rakhi's room and asked her if it was all right for him to sleep with her. Rakhi remembered Dinesh and got very frightened of Anil. She told Anil:

"How dare you talk to me like that? Once, I took care of you when you were a baby. Now being the wife of your elder cousin Rahul I am like your mother. Aren't you ashamed of asking me to allow you to sleep with me? Get out of my room now. I am going to tell Rahul"

"Look, I didn't mean like that. I am feeling lonely and I thought that I could sleep with you in the same bed."

"Please get out of my room."

Anil, aged twenty years, left the room.

Rakhi informed Rahul about the event by phone. Rahul became very anxious and hurried home. Rakhi was very ill, both physically and psychologically. She remained anxious about the events in the house. There were two main reasons. Firstly, Anil falsely accused Rakhi of being ill always, not doing housework, and not looking after herself and Prakash. The fact was that Rakhi remained too ill to do anything. She had injured her spine. Secondly, Rakhi spent a week in Birmingham, with her sister-in-law Reena, wife of Manu. Reena brought up the subject of past issues relating to Rakhi's work which was criticised for various reasons by the family members. Rakhi was only fourteen when she got married. She was very disturbed on her return from Birmingham. Reena's critical views made Rakhi downhearted. On top of that, Anil's adverse comments about her really stressed her out. He stated that all the tensions in the house were due to her. He openly accused her of being a stupid woman who not only created the tense atmosphere but had lowered the credibility of the family. His language was foul and insulting.

Anil's slightly bowed legs and flat feet tired him easily. He had these defects from his birth. He was prescribed special shoes to help his feet feel less tired. He couldn't do the housework after his return from the shop. Therefore, he expected Rahul and Rakhi to work on his behalf leaving aside all their work. The atmosphere affected Prakash's academic progress. Anil had imposed strict rules for him. Sometimes, Anil would beat him up for allegedly telling lies. Rahul and Rakhi were not aware of the beatings. Prakash dared not say anything to anyone for the fear of more retaliation. His physical injuries were hardly visible. It was the fear instilled in Prakash that was noticed by Rahul. Anil was warned about it.

Rahul contacted Manu to resolve Anil's problems. Manu came up with the idea of an arranged marriage. Anil's parents in India approved the wedding to an Indian girl born in Britain. One day, Manu came to Rahul's place to put the idea to Anil. He agreed. No sooner, Manu left the house, then Anil said,

"It seems that you and others had discussed about my marriage in my absence. Are you plotting to get rid of me?"

Rahul was surprised to hear that. He said,

"What are you saying? There is no plot to get rid of you."

"Yes, you and Manu Patel have conspired to get rid of me. That's why you have brought up this marriage issue." said Anil. Rakhi stood in a corner of the room. Thereafter, Anil picked a verbal fight. He tried to drag Rakhi into the conflict as usual. Rakhi had anticipated that.

"Do you know that she told you a lie about the bedroom incident on that day? You are mad to believe in anything she tells you. You don't know of the things she did when she was in India; she used to accuse my father for all sorts of things; she is nothing but a fraud and a liar"

"Stop talking like that. She is ill and you should be careful of what you say about her."

"All her problems are the result of your actions. I don't care what you say. The stupid bitch has brought about the downfall of the family" Anil spoke loudly as he quickly got up and slapped Rakhi twice consecutively.

Rahul just froze there. He couldn't take any retaliatory measures. Umesh, a boy student from Bombay, who lived in the house, heard all the foul words, particularly those aimed at Rakhi, came inside the room and told everyone to be calm. He told Rakhi and Rahul to get out for a while. Rakhi was in no state to go out. She had no idea what she was saying and couldn't walk straight. She began to have fits due to hypertension. After a while, Rahul managed to take her out of the room. Rahul drove around local area in his car. Rahul tried to calm Rakhi who cried loudly.

After two hours, Rakhi and Rahul returned home and faced Anil accusing them of taking 200 pounds from his bag. He asked Rahul,

"What have you done with my money? If you can't handle the house money, then you should give me the charge to look after it" He looked very angry and continued, "How I am going to meet my expenses? You are definitely plotting to get rid of me. Well, all of you can get lost; go to Manu and conspire as much as you like. I am now penniless."

"You said that the money was in the bag. I have no idea what happened to it. Remember, we were out. Don't tell me about the missing money." said Rahul.

Suddenly, Anil removed his wallet from his pocket and threw it towards Rahul. The latter caught it and slung it back towards Anil. Next, Anil got very angry and threw the wallet in the air. The money flew all over. He then began to charge towards Rahul who, in turn, held him by his shoulders. Rahul forced him to sit on a sofa. He resisted powerfully and tried to remove Rahul's hands without any success. He began to swear at Rahul. Rakhi entered the room and said,

"You, two brothers, shouldn't behave like this. It doesn't suit you," She then addressed Anil, "He is your elder brother and you should not swear at him. He is as honourable as your father is."

Anil turned towards Rakhi and said,

"You are a stupid bastard and trouble maker," Anil shook violently with all his energy. Rahul managed to keep his hold on him. Rakhi started crying and trembling. Rahul told her,

"This animal is'nt going to listen to your plea; the words are meaningless to him. Please be quiet and go out of the room."

Umesh told Rakhi to stop crying and to sit on the sofa. Anil composed himself straight on the sofa and began to remove the legs of the coffee table nearby fast and furiously. He threw each leg in the air and lifted the top of the table with which he was about to hit Rahul on the head. Rahul pushed him towards the wall and grabbed the tabletop and felt like slamming Anil three or four times. However, he realised that he couldn't do it as his heartbeats were throbbing at a very high rate. He felt motionless. He shed tears and began to hate himself. He suddenly remembered his aunt Devi's last words,

'Rahul my son, look after my Anil in future. That stupid Anil wouldn't listen to or obey anyone.'

Rahul had not realised the agony of a mother at that time. Anil kept starring at Rahul and said,

"I would like to see you hitting me. Go on, hit me and find out what I can do to you. You are nothing but a liar and a thief. Go; get inside the back of your wife, you bastard"

All this time, Umesh didn't interfere; he just listened to the conversation. Suddenly, he got hold of Anil by the scruff of his neck and told him,

"You are angry and saying things you wouldn't say otherwise." Umesh then looked at Rakhi and Rahul and told them not to say anything more. Anil was struggling very hard to release himself from the grip of Umesh's hands. He began to swear at Rakhi and her family members in the lowest form of manner. Umesh yelled,

"You listen to me good, Anil. Rahul and Rakhi are my elders from this moment onward. I warn you now. If you say anything against them and continue to swear at them, I will smash your face. Do you hear me?"

Anil with his frothy mouth and red eyes retaliated,

"You are nothing but a stupid, fucking bastard. You don't even belong to us. Just get out of this house. Who gave you the right to address them as yours? You don't know about her; she is a bloody prostitute. I know that shit well, thousands of time. So you bastard, get out of my way"

Umesh slammed his face hard with a heavy punch and dumped him on the sofa behind. Anil was shaking and gathering energy to say something to Rahul.

"So you keep strangers like him in the house to safeguard your protection. Well, I promise that this sort of thing will not intimidate me. I will throw all of you out of this house because my father paid for it"

"If anyone will get out, it will be you, Anil," said Rahul.

Anil quickly got up from the sofa. He was still furiously shaking with froth dripping from his mouth. He went towards the front door of the house and rushed out, nearly falling down the step outside. He closed the door forcefully, breaking the glass. It made an almighty shattering noise.

Soon, he knocked on the door. Rahul opened it. He came inside charging and said,

"You get out. Why should I? You are the fucking bastard who should vacate this house. My father paid money to you."

Anil had no knowledge of the method of the house purchase. Rahul never found it necessary to discuss such details with him.

Rahul and Rakhi went into the bedroom. Rakhi made it clear that she didn't want Anil in the house. Prakash walked in the room crying. He had witnessed lot of things downstairs. He hugged Rakhi who started to cry also. Rahul felt guilty of not doing something in return for the slaps Rakhi received earlier. He tried to balance the views as an elder of the family. However, Rakhi accused him of being fearful and uncourageous. Rahul was more concerned about Rakhi's health and ensured that there was no animosity in the house. He was frightened of Anil's constant bickering and physical violence threats.

Rakhi's health deteriorated further. She became asthmatic and dependent on ventilator and painkillers and anti depressants. Anil had a field day seeing her in that state. Rahul did his best to look after Rakhi. He faced problems at his workplace regarding frequent absence and demand for leave. He worried about Prakash generally because the boy had seen enough things that affected his thinking. Praksh's school reports showed his poor performance in most subjects and lack of home work. A psychologist examined Rakhi's situation and concluded that she needed a change of place.

Manu became aware of the situation; He got in touch with Dinesh for consent to have Anil married to a girl born in the UK. The girl, aged twenty, had left the school and worked in a department store. After the marriage, Anil claimed a British passport. They resided in the flat above the shop. A few years later, his elder brother Suresh took up residency in the USA. Later, Anil burnt his shop at night by short circuiting the electrical wires so that he could claim money from the insurance company. He pretended that he knew nothing about the cause of fire. The insurance company discovered the cause of fire. The court issued a warrant for the arrest of Anil. He, by then, had disappeared with his family to the USA.

Rakhi never recovered from the shock of the accusations made by almost every member of the family. Dinesh brainwashed all in the family with his opinion that Govind family, and, in particular Rakhi, were untrustworthy. Dinesh acquired all the properties and money that belonged to Govind.

After all the events, Dinesh became more power hungry. He imposed his will in every way on the members of the family. He became disrespectful to his father and mother ever since Rahul's departure for England. Jogi and Mani, being more dependent on Dinesh for money, were afraid of him.

With the amassed wealth, Dinesh began to take an interest in politics. He donated large sums of money to the political party he supported. He gave money generously to school building projects. With his outside activities increased, he paid cursory attention to family life and the problems therein. He maintained strict financial control over the household expenditure. The children were extremely frightened of him. They dared not get involved in any activities without his express approval.

Once, Suresh drove cousins in the family car to the school without Dinesh's knowledge. When the latter found out about it from the headmaster of the school, he locked the boys up in room and instructed the family members not to give any food and water to them for the day. His younger brother Ghirdhar acted as his account manager.

When the boys and the girls began to attend universities, he kept vigilant attention on their activities and expenditures. This sort of control bred lies and cheats amongst the boys and girls. Once, the boys took the family car to attend a party in the nearby city without the permission and knowledge of the uncle and Dinesh. The car got involved in a major accident due to high speed driving at night. The off side front wing received severe damage which meant that they had to have the repairs done before returning home. The boys were panicking. Then, one of them remembered his friend who was a professional car repairer. They arrived in the friend's village in the early hours of the morning and requested for the repairs to be done urgently. They paid a heavy price for the work before heading home.

The reception committee was waiting for their arrival in the morning. Dinesh was standing in front of the other family members. He was smoking heavily and very angry as the boys came out of the car. The eldest boy, Suresh took the responsibility to be the spokesperson.

"Welcome home, prince. Hope you enjoyed the ride and whatever you did." Dinesh made the remarks.

The boys were shivering. The representative was sweating and shaking. He braved to say,

"We are a little late because the party went on for a little longer".

Dinesh noticed the steam coming out of the front of the car. It was hot and he could feel the heat from the engine.

119

"At what speed did you drive the car? Dinesh enquired.

"Drove a little fast because we were getting late"

"You could have stayed in a hotel," remarked Dinesh. His younger brother, Girthar said,

"Go, all of you, get inside the house."

The boys got inside the house hurriedly. Dinesh turned around towards his brother and said,

"You are the one who spoils them. I suggest you suspend their allowances for a week. That is the way to stop them from lying." Dinesh walked away in disgust from the scene and the rest of the members went inside the house.

Later on, Girthar enquired about the trip. Suresh disclosed all the facts. He added that he told lies because of the fear of reprisal. He promised that no one in future would do such thing again. Girthar looked at them for a few seconds and told them to get on with their work. The leader expressed his concern about the allowances.

"Don't worry. I will think of something." Girthar said. That was a big relief for the boys.

Thus, a breeding ground for telling lies arose because of Dinesh's attitude.

THE TURNING POINT

PRAKASH MEETS SEEMA

As the car sped on the motorway towards Dudley, Rakhi couldn't contain her enthusiasm at the prospect of bringing home a new daughter-in-law. She would treat her as her own daughter and give her all the training in the household duties. It was a known fact that some girls born in the western world would have very little knowledge about a Gujarati family's traditional ways. Rakhi turned to Rahul and said,

"You just wait and see how I will guide her slowly into doing things the way we do. I knew nothing about cooking and house work at the time of our marriage. Ma and Ba guided me on all those things I became expert in. Since we have no daughter, I will treat her like my daughter. You see a daughter always will look after parents, no matter where she is and whatever condition she is in. I will teach her all about Gujarati cooking. I will have the meals ready when they come home from work. As you know, they have to work very hard at their place of work"

"That would be nice but come down to the real world. Don't get carried away now. Remember your uneven heartbeats and asthma condition. You don't want to inflame them, do you?" Rahul looked at Rakhi who didn't answer. He continued,

"Don't you think that your approach could hamper their other plans? She may not take an interest in cooking and house cleaning. Then, what will you do? She may feel dog tired at the end of a day's hard work. Stop dreaming and bear in mind that we will have to know first what type of girl she is"

"She is young and I am confident that she will agree to learn most things" Rakhi's face reflected the majestic look as she remained in her dream world.

In 1986, it was an important turning point in their life. Prakash, aged 23 wasn't ready to get married. He wanted to pursue further study that would qualify him to take up an estate agency business. He remained non committal on the marriage issue like many boys of his time. However, as he was considerate about the family matters, he weighed up the health situation of his parents. Both struggled hard throughout their life. If they were to continue further, all in the family would face serious consequences, financially and health wise. Prakash worked in an estate agency firm. His salary helped to put the family on a better financial footing. There was social pressure on his family to have him married, as everyone, nearest and dearest, was concerned about Rakhi's health. Anil's offensive accusations had left a damaging imprint on Rakhi's mind. Having seriously considered these circumstances, Prakash declared his intention to get married.

"Why are you thinking suddenly of marriage?" Rakhi asked.

"Look at you, mum. You are not well. I see you struggling to cook and keep the house tidy every day. Dad works hard and he comes home very tired too. Then, seeing you doing things generally when your health is poor, he feels for you and does a lot of work in the house too. When I come home from work, I notice both of you have done a lot of work; I feel sad and try to help. Wouldn't it be nice to have someone who could help you in the house? So, I thought that I should get married hoping that my wife will help you to do the house work too."

Rakhi painfully realised the sacrifice that Prakash was willing to make. Rahul and Rakhi had high hopes that he would pursue further studies at advanced level. However, both accepted that he wouldn't be able to, due to circumstances in the house. They believed that Prakash could study further after the marriage if he so wished.

Rakhi was happy. She hugged Prakash and said,

"Do you have a girl in mind?"

Prakash was shy by nature when it came to having a friendship with a female. He had a close friendship with a girl. He said,

"I know one Gujarati girl with whom I have been very friendly. For your information, I tell you that she is not of the Patel cast. (This cast originally migrated from north of Gujarat hundreds of years ago. Historically speaking, this cast was awarded the title 'PATEL' meaning Headman or village chief, by the then ruling king to collect taxes.) She belongs to the Lohana community (Historically known as the masters of sword/ warriors but now in trading business). She is very considerate and kind girl. Her mother taught her about cooking and social etiquette. I have found out lately that my good friend Pankaj is going out with her.

So, I am prepared to get married to another suitable girl. How does that sound to you, mum?"

"That is great, my son. I will ask my brother, Kiran, to find a girl for you." Rakhi hugged him again.

Rahul and Rakhi arrived at Kiran's house in Dudley. It was a two bedroom terraced house with its front door opening onto the level with the pavement. The door led to a small living room; from there a side corridor lead to another room at the back and a small kitchen. The front room was used as a storage place for furniture, beds and miscellaneous household things. The back room was used for dining, seating and general utility purpose. A coal fire in the room was the main source of heating. There was no central heating in the house. A door at the back of the kitchen led to the outside toilet and shower shed. The dull faded yellow wallpaper had come off the walls in places due to damp. The dining-cum-seating room smelt of cooking, drying clothes and cigarette smoke.

Kiran was thin young man with dark skin tone. He was a talkative and tenacious person. He never took an interest in learning English after arriving from India in 1962. He began to work in a local factory making trousers and shirts but soon gave up the job as he got very tired after a day's work. Chhotu, his elder brother had bought the house when Kiran came to Dudley. After his brother had gone to live in India, Kiran took over the house and lived with his wife Kamini and daughters Parul and Kanta. The family lived on benefits. The girls, whose names were chosen from the list of community names, attended the local schools.

Kiran had joined an agency doing the business of money exchange with India and some countries in Africa. As an agent, he collected English pounds here from people who wanted to send money to their relations in those countries. He gave more of local currencies of the countries than the official rate of exchange. He had contacts with business people abroad who wanted to deposit sterling in their accounts in the UK. They needed foreign exchange to do business with the UK manufacturers. Their respective governments had imposed restrictions on the sterling allowances for the overseas business. Kiran got a certain percentage of commission on every transaction he handled. He accumulated his commissions of the local currencies in the respective countries and expanded his business in foreign exchange of money from his own funds overseas. Thus, he was making good money out of his illegal transaction business. He was aware of the danger of getting caught by the authority but continued his business. He knew of other people doing similar business.

Rahul and Rakhi went to Dudley to meet Kiran; there they informed Kiran that Prakash was ready to get married. Rahul said,

"A relative suggested seeing a girl of the family living in Leeds. The father's name is Jivan. Do you know this person?"

Kiran said,

"I do know him and his family; they have good credibility, both here and in India. Jivan is working as a supervisor in an electronic company. His wife, Lata works in a local factory and the two daughters, Seema and Sital are in a college still. The eldest Seema, you are interested in, is pursuing a course of accountancy. She is very pretty and smaller than Prakash. My elder brother Chhotu's son, Vasant attends the same class in the college where she studies. I think this is a suitable girl for Prakash. Should you take further interest in this matter, let me know so that I can arrange a date to see the girl." Kiran's face lit up as he felt happier to get involved in this matter. It would create strong bond between Jivan and himself which would help his exchange business. He didn't charge for arranging the marriage link. He preferred goodwill.

"Since you know them so well, we will talk to Prakash about this and let you know. Meanwhile can you find out about her date of birth and the place where she was born?" said Rahul.

Kiran said,

"I know her date of birth is 13th August 1968. She was born in Leeds. I think her given name is based on the position of stars and time of her birth. However, I will make sure of that and let you know when you agree to proceed further."

"OK, we will let you know". After dinner, Rahul and Rakhi returned home.

Rakhi was over the moon about having a daughter-in-law in the house. Rahul remained cautious. Both were aware that most of the time, there was a personal motive involved of the third party, be it a brother or a friend, in arranging a marriage. They knew that Kiran dealt in money exchange business, but weren't aware of Kiran's interest in ongoing business deals with Jivan. They put their trust in Kiran's investigation and decided to consult the members of their respective families in the villages Pinsad and Sakri in India. Dinesh informed Rahul that he checked out with the family relations of Jivan and Rakhi's father who was well-known for arranging marriages.

Both parties had given good reports on the credibility of Jivan's family in the UK. Dinesh consulted also a trusted priest to find out if the stars under which Prakash and Seema were born were indicative of a good match in every respect. The priest, who had not seen both, said that the couple was a good match. Seema would be very charming and intelligent girl and Prakash would be handsome and considerate. He would progress tremendously in some business. After consulting the latest Panchhang, an astrological book containing information on birth signs, time and day, the priest provided the traditional marriage charts for both. The rectangular charts, marked in red, contained drawings of the positions of stars and some numerical figures. The details of the relevant dates were inscribed in red too. The chart made for Prakash was retained in his house. The one prepared for Seema was delivered later by the family priest, dressed up in brand new white shirt and white cotton 'DHOTI' to Rahul's family as the invitation for marriage.

Rakhi didn't trust much of what Dinesh had told them as she trusted her father's report. Upon receipt of the reports, Rahul and Rakhi asked Kiran to arrange a date and time for seeing Seema in her house in Leeds.

On the appointed day, Rahul, Rakhi and Prakash drove to Kiran's house in Dudley. From there, they were accompanied by Kiran and his wife, Kamini and Vasant. As the two cars headed towards Leeds, Rakhi began to give some advice to Prakash when seeing Seema.

"Don't ask awkward questions and don't frighten the poor girl. Make sure you know about her education and what she would want to do after the marriage. Of course, find out if she can cook our Indian food and likes wearing saris. I know that you young people don't like us in our traditional costumes, walking together with you, because you feel ashamed when the curious English people look at us."

Rahul interrupted her to express his views.

"My dear Rakhi, don't you think Prakash knows that? Stop getting carried away with the subject."

"Oh, you keep quiet, what do you know about the behaviour of modern young boys and girls when they meet for the first time? Haven't you heard about one girl who asked the boy if he had any dustbins in the house, meaning his old parents? Then she suggested further that she would marry on condition that the old people lived separately from them. What good is there in having such a silly girl as your daughter-in-law? They go for the external looks of one another and immediately fall for the dreamy infatuated life style."

"Didn't we do that when we met for the first time?" Rahul said as he winked at Prakash.

"Like hell we did! I tell you Prakash, he was standing miles away from me and I had to move closer to him when we first met" Rakhi expressed with annoyance.

"You two, be quiet please. I will ask about her education, her hobbies, and what she likes to wear etcetera OK? I will also ascertain if she likes cooking and doing house work. Moreover, I will tell her about your health so that she would know that she would be expected to take good care of you." Prakash clarified some points to assure Mum. Rakhi suddenly went very quiet as the car stopped in front of Jivan's semi detached three bedroom house. It was located in a quiet residential area. A small garden patch in the front was safeguarded by a brick wall.

A petite, lovely looking girl with a broad smile revealing two dimples, one on either side of her cheeks, opened the front door of the house. Rakhi and others approached the girl and greeted her. Prakash was the last one to enter. He smiled at the girl unsure that she was the one they had come to see. The girl's mother, Lata welcomed them. They sat in the small living room with bay window. Three-seaters and one single-seater burgundy coloured sofas nearly filled the room. The floor was covered with well used blue carpet. The faded greyish coloured wall paper and furniture were in need of replacing. One single light bulb hung from the middle of the ceiling. A gold coloured metal stand with three small lights stood in one corner. The air in the room smelt of fried oil despite an open window.

Prakash sat next to Vasant who knew Seema very well as they studied in the same class in school. There was another girl in the family and Prakash didn't know which one was for him to see. Vasant pointed at Seema who had opened the front door.

Lata and her younger daughter, Sital brought some tea, fruit juices and spicy snacks and offered the items to everyone. Seema joined in to offer drinks to Vasant and Prakash. The latter was dazzled by her awesome facial beauty. His drink glass nearly slipped from his hand. Rahul and Rakhi had a good close look at Seema as she approached Prakash. Seema gave a broad smile to Vasant and said,

"How are you? I haven't seen you in the classroom for a while."

"Hadn't been well. I had tummy ache."

Again, Rahul and Rakhi took an interest in what Seema was saying. They paid attention to her sweet voice and admired her dimples as they began to sip the tea. Jivan who sat close to Rahul asked,

"How long have you been in the UK, Mr. Patel?"

"I have been here since 1955 and Rakhi joined me in 1961"

"Oh, so you have been here long before we came from Tanganyika. I hear you are working in the Customs at the airport."

"Yes, I joined the department in 1975 after spending twelve years in another government department in the city of London"

"You have a very respectable and powerful job. I work as a supervisor in the ELCO electronic company here in Leeds." They continued talking about other things.

Seema and Prakash went upstairs to a bedroom. Seema shut the door. It had King Size bed; one side wall was completely covered with white cupboards and mirrors. Two small lamp stands stood on side cabinets. The large bay window lit up the room with outside bright light. Seema who sat on the dressing table's stool, fired the first question,

"Do you have a sister?"

"No. Not in my family. We have a very close family friend who has two daughters. They accept me as their elder brother. I see you have one younger sister, what is her name?"

Prakash stood up from the bed, adjusted his jacket as he walked down to the edge of the bed to see in the mirror that the back of his jacket was OK. He then sat at the end of the bed. Seema admired his handsome body covered in gray striped outfit. She said,

"Sital, she is two years younger than I am. She attends a school nearby."

"Vasant told me that you are doing accountancy. Is it for a CA or some other course? You see, I don't know much about the subject" Prakash smiled as he said that.

"It's OK; sometimes I feel that way too. I am doing a diploma course in accountancy"

"Well, I have taken a few 'A' levels and want to do a degree course" said Rahul.

"Oh, Vasant told me that you were working in an estate agency"

"That is true. I thought I should get some experience in that field as I might go for that profession in future. Also, it helps to bring some money in the house. My parents work very hard. My father often comes home very late if he was conducting an interview in the work place."

"I have taken a temporary clerical job as I do part time study."

"What are your sideline interests?" asked Rahul.

Seema smiled as she looked at Prakash and said,

"Yes, I like shopping and lots of money for that."

Prakash made a mental note of her interest. He continued,

"I like modern outfits too. I have to budget my expenditures. I don't rely on my father's income as long as I can. I also play musical instruments like Tabla(Drums) and keyboard. My main interest is in motorcars."

"Tell me about your parents."

"My father came here in 1955 and followed education up to Bsc. Economics degree at the London University. My mother came to this country in 1961. She mainly looks after us and the house. She had injured her back when she fell down the stairs. After my birth, my uncle from Africa joined our family. After few years he left us. My mother's health is not very good. My father works in the customs, as you probably know from your father." All this time, Prakash admired her smile and dimples and frequent flicks of her front few curly hairs she made. He was hooked and smiled every time he spoke to her.

He asked Seema about her parents,

"My father came here with his brother from Tanganyika in 1958. My mother followed soon. My father works as a supervisor in the local electronic company and my mother works in a factory near our house. We are two sisters and I am the eldest."

"What would you like to do in future?" Prakash asked, anticipating possible marriage with her.

"I want to take up a full time job in the accountancy field after my course is over. My father knows some people in that line of business. I imagine he will try to get a well paid job for me. We don't mingle with many of our society people. Most of them are very old fashioned and believe in superstitions. They interfere too much in our life. We have a large number of relations. They live in Leeds and Nottingham. We celebrate parties and festive occasions among ourselves."

"Would you be able to look after my parents? My mother needs help in doing housework and the cooking. She is an excellent cook."

"Of course, I will help her." Seema reluctantly replied. By her nature that was cultivated by her mother she didn't like to serve others.

She anticipated Rahul's mother overseeing her and Seema being a very independent person never liked to be in that situation. Prakash noted that Seema wasn't smiling. A cloud of seriousness had covered her face.

"Are you a vegetarian? I eat veg and non-veg food. My parents are pure vegetarians." Prakash asked.

"I eat chicken, sausages and bacon. I also like the non-veg food you get in the restaurants. I can cook non-veg food but not so much of the Indian stuff."

Prakash thought that his mum would teach her about cooking Indian food. After all his family ate home—cooked vegetarian food every day.

Lata sent Sital upstairs to see if Prakash and Seema had concluded their introductory talk. When she knocked on the door,

"We will be down in a minute." Seema replied.

A few minutes later, both came down. As Prakash sat next to Rahul, he winked at Rakhi suggesting that he liked the girl. Seema and Lata went into the kitchen where Seema pointed out that the boy was OK but he wanted her to look after his parents forever.

"Seema, if you think he likes you than we will wait for their reply. They are not going to commit themselves right now. I will tell your papa about this. After they leave, we will talk about the interview in detail. They seem well to do people. Don't worry about looking after the parents. We will sort that issue out in the end."

They left the kitchen and joined the others in the lounge. Kiran talked about some clients who wanted to deposit money with Jivan. Rahul and Rakhi just sat listening to Lata's conversation with Sital who was about to go to school. About fifteen minutes later, Kiran suggested that they should head for home.

Rahul, Rakhi and Prakash had the evening meal with Kiran's family. Rahul and Rakhi informed Kiran that they would await Jivan's decision.

On the way back home, Prakash asked Rakhi,

"Mum, how did you feel when you saw dad for the first time in Navsari?"

"I liked your dad straight away because I felt instantly that he was the chosen one for me. Anyway, why do you ask? She turned the sun visor down and looked at Prakash through the vanity mirror.

Prakash's face was beaming with happiness. He said,

"Mum, I felt the same way about Seema".

Rahul also glanced at Prakash through the visor mirror and said,

131

"Son, you be careful jumping to conclusions; looks are not everything, analyse in detail what she said during the interview. We will talk about it tomorrow."

Prakash sat back in silence. Rakhi said,

"Do you think she will adopt our style of living? I noticed that her family members were speaking Gujarati in a slightly different way."

"Oh, Rakhi, what can Prakash say about Seema's performance? He can't pronounce Gujarati words properly. This is a different generation we are dealing with. I wish you wouldn't rush into this matter." Rahul wanted to stop Rakhi excitedly carrying on with the subject.

AFTER THE MARRIAGE

Rakhi was full of enthusiasm. Soon after the marriage, every morning she expected Seema and Prakash to come downstairs for breakfast. It consisted of cereals, porridge, spiced up potatoes and rice flakes snack, tea and offee. Seema hardly indulged in any conversation. She wouldn't even smile. Rahul and Rakhi thought that it was perhaps due to different customs and given time, she would adjust. Rahul said,

"Make sure that you don't interfere with their life. I see you're all geared up to instruct her on various things like cooking, cleaning and socialising. You know, I have this gut feeling that her entire family is not very keen on meeting people. When we met them before the marriage, I tried to find out about their views on society and hobbies etc. I said,

"Jivan Patel, what's your view of the Indian families living here? Are they sociable?"

"We try to keep a distance from them because they want to know everything about us. They often disapprove of my girls, who in their view are too westernized. They think the children should learn about Indian culture also. We do try to teach them something about our culture but the girls speak in English as they talk in their schools all the time."

"Do you and your daughters have any hobbies?"

"I take interest in TV and household repairs. The girls like to do shopping and give some help in the house work. The girls, due to lack of Indian cultural upbringing, grew up as 'English'. We socialise with our nearest relatives only. We hold parties amongst ourselves; the outsiders weren't invited."

Jivan's family assumed that Prakash's family was wealthy. Rahul and Rakhi weren't aware of that. Lata was determined to see that Seema acquired wealth to lead her life independently after the marriage. Under social pressure Jivan's family agreed to arrange the marriage.

Rakhi said,

"Oh, even I noted that Lata didn't know much about our traditions. If she had no knowledge of and interest in cultural traditions how can we expect Seema to know about them? I think Seema will adjust to our life-style as the time goes by. She is young and will soon pick up our ways." Rakhi stated of her firm belief. She was aware of herself that she had no experience of domestic work when she got married. She learnt all by experience at her in-laws' place as the time passed by.

"I am not too sure if that would apply to Seema. Anyhow, leave it to Prakash. You remain careful; don't force her to do things" Rahul concluded.

Prakash and Seema decided to go to Barbados for their honeymoon. Prakash was willing to go anywhere but Seema's parents, who had visited Barbados, suggested that they go to Barbados. Seema liked that suggestion.

When Rahul enquired about the cost of the trip, Prakash said,

"Dad, at the wedding, I received approximately one thousand two hundred and fifty pounds cash as gifts from people. We would like to spend a week there. We have looked at the holiday package offered by Thomas Cook and found that we would require at least two thousand five hundred pounds. The price includes everything like airfares, accommodation, food and sight-seeing tours."

Rahul and Rakhi remained silent for a while. Seema sat quietly on the nearby chair looking at Prakash. Her facial expressions reflected doubt of getting financial help.

"Let us think over about it" Rahul said as he and Rakhi got up and made their way to the bedroom upstairs.

"How are we going to find the extra money?" Rakhi expressed her concern.

"Having borrowed fifteen thousand pounds for the wedding, it's going to be difficult to raise the extra money. We don't want to borrow any more money from the bank or friends" Rahul explained the situation.

"Hey, wait a minute, can't they go to places like Tenerife or Malaga or Paris or Rome?" Rakhi suggested.

"Don't be naïve, Rakhi. They decide where they want to go for honeymoon. You and I can't tell them to go somewhere else!"

"Sorry, that's true" said Rakhi. She continued, "I can persuade Prakash secretly to go somewhere cheaper."

"Oh, you can't do that. It's their privilege to choose the place for their honeymoon. I don't think you should say anything to Prakash. Think how we can help them to have their unique event fulfilled."

After deliberation, Rakhi said,

"During the wedding, we received money as presents too. Didn't you deposit that in our savings account? What's the total savings we have?" She looked at Rahul.

"Hey, just a minute, darling; its good thinking on your part." Rahul got up from the bed and fetched the savings book from the cupboard.

"I deposited eight hundred pounds, making a total savings of one thousand two hundred and fifty pounds. We could give thousand pounds to them." said Rahul

"Yes. That would leave two hundred fifty pounds in the account. What if there is an unexpected need for more money? Where will we get it?" Rakhi hesitated.

"Well, what else can we do? We will take the chance and somehow we will borrow if necessary in the future. I suppose I will have to do more overtime." Rahul said.

Both were unhappy in parting with the large chunk of their savings but on the other hand, they wanted Seema and Prakash to have the best.

At breakfast time, Rahul informed Prakash and Seema that they could have the extra money. They had to find the balance of two hundred fifty pounds.

"It's OK dad. Seema has some money. Actually, her dad wanted to pay the total cost of the trip but I decided not to have that." Prakash said.

"Quite right too, Prakash" said Rakhi, "We shouldn't put a burden on Jivan Patel by accepting his offer. It isn't done in our society"

On their arrival from Barbados, Rakhi asked,

"Seema, did both of you have a good time?

"It was alright. He kept on complaining that I spent more time looking in the shop windows." Seema, with sullen facial features replied halfheartedly about their trip. She made a quick exit from the living room and went upstairs.

Prakash disclosed some aspects of Seema's behaviour he observed during the holiday.

"I don't know but she appeared to be very demanding. She wanted to buy many expensive things for her parents and sister. She never mentioned anything for you. When I suggested about gifts for you, she kept on telling me that it was up to me. She didn't show any enthusiasm for you two. In the end, she bought small things like necklaces and purses for her family and nothing for you. Later, I thought perhaps she was right. What did she know about you and your likes? So, I just got the leather handbag for mum. Sorry dad, I couldn't find anything for you."

"We noticed she isn't cheerful and cooperative at home too. Is there a problem with her? I think you should find out about this. We want her to be happy in our family." said Rahul.

Jivan and Lata frequently visited Rahul's house to spend most of their time with Seema. They took her shopping and ate outside. At first, Rakhi cooked food for them assuming that they would have it at her home. Upon their return, when Rakhi began to set up the table for lunch, Lata said that Jivan was very hungry so they'd eaten in a restaurant.

Rakhi was annoyed,

"You should have informed me that you were to have lunch outside. I prepared food for you and now we will have to eat it as dinner, I am afraid".

There was no response from them. Lata smiled a little as she looked at Seema and Jivan. The latter reciprocated with their smile.

Seema visited her parents once a fortnight. Her father bought a second hand car for her and delivered it to Rahul's house. Rahul was concerned about the total expenditure for three cars in the family. He said to Jivan,

"Three cars are expensive to maintain. Seema could share the car with Prakash. Moreover, I could assist her whenever she needed to go out."

"We wouldn't mind assisting our daughter for the car expenses. She needs her freedom to go out whenever she wants to" Lata jumped in showing a little anger on her face in Seema's defence.

Rahul, Rakhi and Prakash were stunned by Lata's statement.

Rahul said,

"Mr. Patel, you know the tradition that after the marriage, she shouldn't expect any assistance from you. The responsibility lies with us to meet all her needs."

Seema snapped back,

"I need a car. I can't wait for anyone to provide transport whenever I need to go out. That is why papa bought the car for me. Neither Prakash nor you can afford to buy a car for me. What's wrong in getting my parents' help?"

Again, Rakhi and Rahul looked at each other with surprise. They began to note the characteristics of Seema and tried to seek the reason for her behaviour. In a way, they both felt insulted by Seema's attitude towards many things in the house. She became awkward in many respects about things; she would rearrange flower vases, mirrors, insisted on having expensive replacement of window curtains. In particular, Rakhi was affected mentally by her inept remarks on many occasions. For example, if Rakhi suggested vegetable Dal and rice for lunch, Seema would say,

"I don't like that kind of food. You lot can have it if you want. I will cook food I like." She normally ate spiced corn, chicken bits, curried pigeons beans and potatoes and onion rings.

"OK. We all will have what you cook."

"I am in a hurry and I will grab something from the high street shop. You can cook what you like."

Rakhi wasn't happy. She wanted her to eat home cooked food. Seeing Seema's slightly angry mood, Rakhi felt annoyed but said nothing.

One evening, after dinner, all except Seema who went to her room upstairs, sat in the living room to decide whether or not they all should attend a pre-wedding ceremony in a relative's house in Ilford. Seema knew about the wedding invitation from Ilford.

Prakash called Seema to join in the decision making. The invitation was for all of them. Seema came running down and stood near the door and said sharply,

"If you are talking about the wedding in Ilford, I don't want to go. You can go. I don't know them." She was abrupt; her voice sounded positive and very determined.

"Beti (daughter), these are very close relatives of our family. We all have to attend the ceremony. You will like the people."

"If I don't know them, what is the point in going there? In any case, I don't like to waste time on silly traditional ceremonies. I get bored to tears. You lot can go. I am not coming." She stood near the door, looking at the floor. She wore blue jeans and a black top.

Prakash looked at his parents and said,

"Leave it to me, please. We'd like to think it over."

Both Prakash and Seema went upstairs. Rakhi appeared concerned,

"How are we going to deal with this daughter-in-law of ours? She retorts back without due respect and seems very unwavering about everything we say. What will happen to our son?"

"Now don't you go worrying about it? She will come to understand most things as the time goes by." Rahul tried to reassure Rakhi.

"The trouble lies with you. You don't have the guts to lay authority whenever there are such problems. You should have backed me when I said that we have to attend the ceremony. But, you just sat there saying nothing. Seema will blame me for being bossy to her. I don't know why she is acting like that. During the day time, when you and Prakash are at work, she doesn't speak to me. When I say to her,

"Seema, make sure all the tiny stones and such foreign substance from the cereal are removed. If you have some time, please grind the dried coriander also, we are running short of it."

"I can't do both today. I have no time nor interest for this kind of work. People buy readymade coriander and other cereals. Why can't we do the same? We don't have to make fuss about readymade items."

Rakhi seemed frustrated. She began to perspire a lot and found breathing difficult. Rahul fetched water for her.

"See, by worrying too much, you run short of breath and begin to perspire. I don't think this is good for you. What do you say?" Rahul knew that she was seriously affected by Seema's attitude towards her. Both went to their room. Rakhi closed her eyes and lay in bed. Rahul noticed a few tears in her eyes. He realised that Rakhi was telling the truth but he was at a loss to find the solutions too about the problems created by Seema's attitude.

By now, Seema considered Rakhi as an old fashioned and illiterate woman who followed old traditions blindly without knowing the real meanings of them. In contrast, Seema believed that she was a modern woman, by virtue of having been educated in England and having the experience of a modern life-style. She didn't like wearing a sari everyday Rakhi never suggested that she should wear a sari every day. Seema preferred black jeans and a short sleeved top, to traditional Indian dress. Rakhi had no qualms about it but insisted that when attending Indian functions, it would be nice if Seema wore saris or a Punjabi salwar kameez suit.

Prakash tried to convince Seema that following certain traditional Indian things was necessary for our old people. He began to explain to her, "My parents grew up with those traditions and consider it necessary to follow them. That was the way they led their life. I suppose we will be doing the same thing in our old age. Mind you, not all traditions are bad for us. For example, I find it quite hilarious when a brother of the bride steals the groom's shoes while they are on the stage during the wedding. Later, the brother demands money from the groom for the return of his shoes. Don't ask me why this sort of thing happens, but I find it funny. Don't you?"

Seema remained busy doing something to her top. After deliberation, she spoke,

"I don't mind traditional things but your mum is blinded by any tradition of India. When is she going to learn about the modern ways of life? Why can't she wear a Punjabi suit? It is perfectly respectable, covers the body well."

"Seema darling, you haven't seen the progress she has made ever since she came in this country in 1961. Dad often told me about her frustration resulting from not knowing English, her difficulty doing shopping by herself and the feeling of aloofness and loneliness at the parties thrown by English friends. He gave her a basic alphabet book for learning the language when he went to work. She, and to a certain extent even dad, will not know perfect English as they spent their youths in India. Isn't it a universal truth that we condition our thinking process to the teachings we have in our early years of life? They grasped everything in Gujarati just as we do in English. I think there should be a compromise approach on every occasion. Does this make sense?" Prakash asked.

"It may do. However, I am not going to waste my time learning things that are of no use to me. All I know is that following certain Indian traditions suffocates me. I dislike the talk of traditions your mum makes every day. That's why I prefer to go out window shopping to avoid the headache. Do you really know anyone well in the family in Ilford? What will you be doing there? I expect we'll have to sit on the crowded floor for hours where the ceremony takes place. Your mum will start introducing me to others and talking about my parents and sisters and which village we came from. Why does she have to do all that?" asked Seema.

Prakash realised that it was going to be a hard job to alter Seema's thinking on traditional things of India. He began to realise that all those lies he told her about his family's lifestyle and the finances, before his marriage, were going to hurt him. Likewise, Seema began to realise that all the lies she'd spoken for sake of acceptance of the marriage proposal and her promises to look after Prakash's parents in old age, were interfering with the freedom she was so used to. Her parents always consulted Seema about everything that was going on in the family. As she grew up, Seema got used to being asked for her opinion before anything was done. Although Rakhi and Rahul would seek her opinion about things to be done in the house, when a difference of opinion arose, Rahul and Rakhi stuck to their way. Seema felt insulted and ignored by their actions.

One day, Jivan and Lata came unexpectedly to meet Seema and Prakash. The latter was sent to Bournemouth by his department to deal with an issue. When Seema's parents couldn't see Prakash, they decided to stay for the night. Rakhi and Rahul were unaware of this arrangement until late in the evening. Rakhi had provided lunch and afternoon tea but had not prepared anything for dinner. When she knew that the guests were to stay the night, she went in the kitchen to prepare for the evening dinner.

"Mum, don't cook for us. We will be going to see a family friend tonight." Seema shouted from the upper floor. Rakhi walked in the living room and looked at Rahul.

"Did you hear that?" Rakhi stood in front of Rahul; he asked her to sit down. He could see slight perspiration on her head.

"Don't they have a nerve? Do they think we are their servants? Are we to facilitate their convenience?" Rakhi lost her temper and began to cry.

Jivan, Lata and Seema came downstairs and stood near the living room door when Lata said,

"We are going to see someone and will be back at about 10 o'clock tonight. I hope Prakash will be back by then. Please don't bother about our food." They walked out of the main door. Rahul and Rakhi lost their appetite for dinner. They went upstairs to their room.

By half past ten, the guests returned to find that Prakash wasn't in the house. Jivan enquired from downstairs,

"Why isn't Prakash home yet?"

Rahul and Rakhi came downstairs and invited the worried guests to come into the living room. They reluctantly entered and Jivan took a seat while Lata and Seema stood by a sofa. The atmosphere was tense at first. Then, Lata, fumingly said,

"So it's true that Prakash has a girlfriend. People talk about this and we wondered if there was any truth in it. Now we know for sure that he spends time with her and that's why he isn't here at these late hours. How do you think we and Seema feel?"

Rakhi began to get nervous, hearing about Prakash having a girlfriend. Rahul looked at Jivan and said,

"How can you say those things about our son? Doesn't Seema know him well by now? I think it's pathetic to come up with the accusation at this time of night. Prakash doesn't often work late. Seema knows that.

You can stay here near the door until Prakash comes home. I hope you will get a satisfactory answer from him as to why he isn't here. Come on Rakhi, please don't cry because of what these people suspect and say. Let's go upstairs to sleep." Rahul escorted Rakhi to their room.

"Why hasn't Prakash come home? He went early in the morning and should have returned by five o'clock in the evening. Do we have to hear these stupid people's comments in our own house? Who do they think they are? I think we made a bad mistake by having Seema in the house." Rakhi continued crying.

"Shush, my love, I know your feelings now. I told them what I thought was the right thing to say. I am worried about Prakash too. He should have phoned us if he was to be late. He has a mobile phone. I don't know why he hasn't called." Rahul sat on the bed. Rakhi stopped crying. Her breathing became faster. Rahul gave her the ventilator pump and told her to relax and try to sleep. Rakhi took her medication and turned in the bed. Rahul remained awake until two o'clock. He realised that he should have taken Prakash's mobile number. The phone rang in the bedroom. Rahul sat up and took the phone.

"Hello, dad, I'm sorry I couldn't get in touch with you earlier. My car broke down and it took ages for the AA person to come. There is nothing in the vicinity of this place. It's very dark and raining. My mobile battery is flat and there is no public telephone booth either. I know you must be worried to death. Sorry. I am using the AA phone."

"That is OK son. Are you well? Has the car been fixed? Come home as soon as the car is ready. Drive carefully. By the way where are you?" Rahul enquired

"I am on the main road to London from Bournemouth, near Basingstoke. The AA guy just told me that the car's OK. So I will be home in about thirty five minutes. See you soon. Oh, Is Seema asleep?" Prakash asked assuming that she would be asleep.

"Yes, you come home safe. Bye" Rahul put the phone down and looked at Rakhi who woke up to know where Prakash was.

"His car was out of action on the main London road near Basingstoke. The AA person was very late arriving at the place. Prakash's mobile phone was out of action. He is OK and on his way back here." said Rahul.

"I am going downstairs to tell those stupid people off and cook some food for our son. Poor thing, he must be starving by now. There are people in our own house who think he is having good time with some woman."

Rakhi tried to get out of the bed but Rahul held her arm and said,

"No darling, leave everything now. On arrival, he is going to face them downstairs. We will be there also. After hearing them, he is going to tell them a few things. I know my son and what he will do when he is misjudged by anyone."

Rakhi remained in bed.

Prakash arrived home just before two o'clock in the morning. He was tired. As he opened the front door, Lata wasted no time in asking,

"Had a few beers and enjoyed your evening then?"

Prakash was stunned hearing that. He wondered if dad had informed these people about what had happened. He said,

"Not exactly. My car broke down."

"Likely story. From what we have heard, you drink a lot and have a girl friend. You do realise that our daughter is your wife, don't you?" Lata snapped back in anger.

"I think you must be out of your mind. Do you really think I did all those things you said?" Prakash looked angrily at Seema. "My car broke down and the AA guy couldn't come immediately. He appeared on the scene after two hours. Is this the way to welcome me in my own house?" Prakash walked into the living room. Rahul and Rakhi came down stairs and sat on the sofa.

"Are you OK, my son? You look terribly tired. I will get your food ready." spoke Rakhi as she was about to go in the kitchen.

"Look at his eyes, they are red, probably due to drinks he had." remarked Lata.

Prakash looked at Lata and retorted,

"I don't wish to discuss anything with you. Please, go away. It's clearly obvious that you think I drank a lot. Right now, I'm very tired and want to go to sleep. Seema, take your parents upstairs and don't wait for me. I will sleep here. Mum, I am not hungry any more. You too go upstairs."

"You certainly seem to know how to welcome your son-in-law. I'm ashamed to hear you making accusations without concrete evidence. Come, dear, let's retire to our bedroom." Rahul said as he stood up and held Rakhi's hand to escort her upstairs.

Jivan, Lata and Seema remained in the living room. Prakash kept his eyes on them but said nothing. Then, he went upstairs to pick up blankets and a pillow. Meanwhile, Lata said,

"Did you see how angry they got, the moment I spoke about drinks and a girlfriend?"

"They got angry because they couldn't face the truth" Jivan looked at Seema and continued, "Didn't you see from Prakash's behaviour that something was going on in his life?"

"All I know is that he comes home late in the evenings. During the day, he doesn't phone me. Mum keeps on about cooking and cleaning; asking me what I was doing in my room. It isn't her business to know what I do, is it? For your knowledge, I was reading a book. She drives me crazy. I am not interested in her talk about what she and the family members did in the past in India." Seema appeared fed up.

"Seema, my dear, I think you should come and spend some time with us. Just pack up your clothes and we will leave early tomorrow" said Lata. Jivan remained silent. As Prakash came downstairs, they left the room and went upstairs to sleep.

Meanwhile, Rakhi was feeling uneasy and said,

"I am worried. Why should they say all those things about our son? Who could have put these ideas into their minds?"

Rahul could see the features of concern on her face. Worries were reflections of God's punishment, he thought.

"Please, don't worry. I am convinced that our Prakash isn't the sort of boy who would go out with another woman. There must be another reason why these people are acting like this. At work, I was trained to observe the body language of passengers when ascertaining who to stop etc. I learnt to study people's facial look, why they walked hurriedly pulling heavy suitcases etcetera. I didn't like Lata's first statement referring to Prakash's habit of drinking. I could see the nervousness on her face." Rahul lay back in the bed as he noticed Rakhi had fallen asleep.

The following morning, Rahul heard noises coming from Seema's room. He got up and went near the door. He heard a conversation taking place in the room,

"Where are you going so early" asked Prakash. Rahul assumed that Prakash must have gone in the room for something.

"I am leaving this place and going to spend some time with my parents." Seema said.

"Why?"

"I am fed up with being alone in this house." Seema sounded fed up; she suddenly turned the knob of the door. Rahul quickly returned to his room. Seema carried a suitcase downstairs. Prakash followed her and went into the living room where Lata and Jivan were waiting. Prakash looked at them and asked,

"What's going on?"

Lata was quick to reply.

"We think there is no need for Seema to remain in this house. She is coming to stay with us for a while. We will let you know when she is ready to return so you can come to fetch her."

By this time, Rahul and Rakhi joined them in the living room. Prakash looked at Seema and said,

"Is this your idea? If it is, then go. What is it that bothers you in this house? Is it me or something else? Do you really think I have a girlfriend and I am an alcoholic? Think seriously before taking this step, Seema".

"I just want to go away from this house and your mum".

On hearing that, Rakhi said to Seema,

"What have I done to you? Did I get angry at you? Did I make you do things in this house against your will? What is it about me you dislike so intensely?" Rakhi couldn't control her anger and began to cry. She sat down on a chair. Rahul and Prakash could see the pain on Rakhi's face.

"I hope you know what you are doing by taking Seema out of this house. You have falsely accused our son and now Seema blames Rakhi too. Is there anything else for us to face from you?" asked Rahul.

"We have decided to take Seema for a while, that's all" Lata replied.

"Come on, let's go. No point in wasting time here." Seema said as she began to move towards the front door. Prakash, Rahul and Rakhi didn't go to say goodbye to them.

"Prakash, it appears that you don't know what these people are up to. Do you two get on very well? Do you know the reason for Seema's apparent hatred for your mum?" Rahul asked,

"Dad, she doesn't tell me anything about her daily discussion with her mother. I know you don't like her sister staying in our house whenever she comes. I tried to tell Seema to cooperate a little and everything would be ok, but we know that doesn't happen. I am caught between you and her. Frankly, I don't know what to do now." Prakash looked very sad.

"Son, we know how you must be feeling. Let me advise you that you should try to reason with Seema and make sure that you have the upper hand whilst being fair to both sides. At the end of the day, you will have to look after your life. Don't worry about us. I will take care of mum. If the condition remains the same, the end result may turn out bad for both of us." Rahul spoke as he turned towards Rakhi who was crying.

"Rakhi my dear, don't cry please. That's not going to resolve the situation. Until we know the reason for Seema's and her parents' attitude, we can't afford to worry about it." Rahul tried to console Rakhi. No one in the house slept well that night. Prakash received a telephone call from Seema on the following day to say that he should go to her house in a week's time.

"Why should you go to bring her here? They took her away so they should bring her here." Rakhi angrily said to Prakash.

"Mum, don't upset yourself. Let me go because I have a good mind to tell her parents that they shouldn't conspire behind our backs and leave Seema and me alone. This time I am going to open up my mind. If they don't want Seema living with us, that's fine by me. You don't worry about anything." Prakash expressed his views.

"No, you will not talk to them rudely. Avoid things that lead to a divorce situation. Nothing like this has happened in our family and we don't want to be the first one." said Rahul.

Early one morning Prakash left for Leeds. Seema's maternal uncles and their family members were present in Jivan's house. After the initial reception, Jivan started a discussion with Prakash.

"Prakash, we are sorry that you had to come here for Seema. We would like to stress our concern about our daughter who faces ridiculous events created daily by your mum. Your father seems to lack understanding of the modern young person's life style. Admittedly, he, being a customs officer, must be an intelligent and considerate person in his field of work. But, both your mum and dad can't see Seema's point of view. Your mum speaks to her in an insulting manner and Seema can't tolerate that. Your father always takes your mum's side and fails to realise Seema's requirements. Both of you are trying to have a baby but because of your parent's interfering nature, she cannot conceive due to the stress. That isn't good. How can you live under these circumstances? If you don't sort out the problem then we will have to consider taking divorce action. What is your view, Mr Patel? Do you think that what I have said sums up the situation?"

Both of Seema's maternal uncles agreed to what Jivan had said. Prakash got little angry. After deliberation, he looked at Seema and asked,

"Is that your view too, Seema?"

"Well, that is the truth, isn't it? We don't think that you are the main cause of the domestic conflict every day. I can't live in that kind of controlled environment."

Prakash slowly turned towards the uncles and asked them,

"Do you entirely share their views? You wouldn't be afraid if this matter reached to divorce stage, would you?"

The uncles spoke and understood little English. One of them, who worked in an accounts department of a store, expressed his mixed views,

"Prakash, I personally don't think that this is a serious enough matter to warrant a divorce. I think that whatever the problems are, both parties should resolve amicably. Let's not rush hastily. I wish your parents were here today. If there is truth in what Seema reports, then you personally should sort it out. Your father is an intelligent person and I respect him very much. Your mother has welcomed us always. If she is eager to show Seema the things she knows, then Seema has to see the events in the light of your mum's life experience. On the other hand, your mum should realise that she can't coerce Seema all the time to attend matters in her way. Young person like you two, don't approve of the traditional things of India. We know that. There should be compromise between the parties over the issues that affect daily life." said one uncle.

"And you, uncle, what is your view?" Prakash asked the other uncle.

"I agree to what my elder brother has said. It's not good to have extreme difference of opinions in the family."

Prakash looked at Lata and Jivan and began to say,

"I am ashamed to hear your critical views about my parents. Seema and you know very little about us; you seem to be very eager to state what sort of my parents are. You don't live with us in our house and we don't meet that often, so how can you form an adverse opinion about my parents? For those remarks alone, I should walk out from here leaving you to do whatever you want to do. However, accepting your opinions, I could equally say that you are trying to interfere in our lives. What rights have you to tell us how we should live? In the beginning, there will be problems of adjustments in a new family. What was your early life experience under the strict domestic rules in Africa and India? Don't tell me that you had happy independent life-style from the day you both got married. Do you think that your parents approved of all your new ways? So, please don't make adverse comments about my family. You should have done the research about our family before giving your daughter to me. The way things are going, I would be blaming my maternal uncle for suggesting that you were a noble family. As to the daily interferences from my mother, I think you should know that she is never an unkind, inconsiderate, and forceful woman. She gets carried away about cooking, cleaning the house and ironing etc because she likes tidiness and likes to be a clean person. Sometimes, because of her insistences, even I get very angry but that is no reason to call her an interfering and insulting person. It's as simple as that. It's up to you and Seema to think again on the issue. I have come to take her home. So, let me know, Seema, what you want to do." As Prakash finished, Seema started crying uninterruptedly and began to run up the stairs saying,

"You lot can keep the relationship with them if you wish, but I don't want to know them and I couldn't care less about them".

Prakash realised that Seema wasn't prepared to do anything that would improve the relationship. Both uncles expressed unanimously that her behaviour was strange. They looked at Lata and Jivan and enquired if they could throw some light on the issue. There was no reply from either of them. Lata got up and went upstairs. On entering the room, she found Seema crying uncontrollably. Lata approached her in haste and hugged her saying,

"Don't cry my BETI. My brothers didn't help the situation by putting a question to your papa and me. I couldn't think of an answer. Now stop crying and let us think constructively. Remember the objectives for your happy life. Prakash's family is old fashioned but it seems to be wealthy. We both know that by getting hold of money, you will have the controlling power over everyone." Seema wiped her tears and looked at her mum who said,

"You see, the solution is very simple. Go with Prakash. Try to establish slowly your authority in the family. Be gentle with that mother-in-law of yours. How does that sound to you?" Seema nodded in agreement.

They came downstairs. Lata declared that Seema would go with Prakash.

After their arrival at home, Prakash and Seema settled down to their daily work. Rakhi wanted to know about what happened in Leeds. In order for Rakhi not to get concern too much, Prakash said,

"Briefly, they were critical of the occurrences in our house. Seema's maternal uncles presented the balanced views reflecting common understanding on the requirements of all persons' lifestyle in our house. I told them that their critical view of us was suggesting that they haven't taken the trouble to understand us. Their views reflected their prejudicial outlook of our lifestyle and I could have equally criticised them similarly on their lifestyle. Now I hope that all of us would endeavour to change our views and live happily."

Rakhi felt that Prakash wasn't disclosing all that was discussed in Jivan's house. She asked,

"Tell me Prakash, what did they say about us?"

Prakash feared that his mother would insist on knowing about everything that happened in Jivan's house. If he were to disclose all that to his parents, he knew that his father would retaliate strongly to his in-laws and his mother would get depressed. That would lead to further friction between the families.

SEEMA GETS PREGNANT

"Mum, I got good news for you. You are going to be grandmother soon." declared Prakash.

"Oh, my son, that is wonderful news. Have you informed your in-laws?"

"Seema had informed them already." said Prakash without realising the consequences of that fact. Rakhi became unhappy; she expected Seema to inform her first. Rahul tried to explain that she shouldn't expect anything; it brings unhappiness. Rakhi wanted Seema to rest in the house since she became pregnant. Prakash knew that coconut water was good for the health of mother and her unborn child. Rahul and Rakhi visited shops that sold fresh coconuts and ensured a good supply at home. They made sure that Seema drank lots of water. For the first time, Seema obliged.

Lata, Jivan and Sital visited Seema frequently. All were happy. Everybody ate in restaurants and enjoyed the outings and conversations. Rakhi remained very reserved for the fear of her views being misunderstood by Lata. Rahul noticed it and encouraged her to say whatever was relevant to the pregnancy and be free of constrains and tensions.

The baby boy was born on the night of full moon in the hospital where Prakash was born. He weighed seven pounds and had round pink face with black eyes. There were plenty of black hairs on his head. Rakhi had the first opportunity to handle the baby when she and Rahul visited the ward. Rakhi held the boy gently and ran her fingers over his head. She looked at Rahul and said,

"Dear, do you remember your photo taken when you were a baby?"

"Yes, I do remember, darling" said Rahul.

"Come and look at this wonderful baby's face. It looks somewhat like your face in that photo." said Rakhi.

Rahul gently took the baby in his hands and observed the face and smiled a little. He then looked at Seema who was in the bed and said,

"Do you think so, Seema? Does he have the face similar to mine?" Rahul asked as he kept the boy's face next to his chin.

"Not really, it's too early to say anything about his face. It will change every day." Seema smiled a little as she replied.

Lata and Jivan rushed straight to Seema and the baby. Lata kissed Seema and said,

"Congratulation. How are you, Beti? Was there much pain during the caesarean section?"

"I was sedated so I felt very little pain. But now I am beginning to feel more pain. I am OK anyway." said Seema.

Seema admired the flowers held by Sital. They were put in a vase placed on top of the cabinet near the bed. Lata took the baby from the hands of Rakhi and gave a big smile and said,

"Look, what a beautiful baby boy this is. He is heavy; what is the weight, Seema?"

"Seven pounds."

Looking at the face of the baby, Lata said,

"He looks like his father, doesn't he, Jivan?"

Jivan moved closer to Lata and took the boy and held in his hands. The baby started to cry. Everyone laughed. Jivan bounced him gently but that made the baby cry more. He handed the boy to Seema who put him next to her on the bed. Soon the baby stopped crying.

A nurse approached Seema with a small bottle of milk. Rakhi enquired if Seema had difficulty in breast feeding. Lata quickly replied, on behalf of Seema,

"I didn't breast feed my two daughters so I advised Seema to do the same."

Rakhi was surprised and looked at Rahul and Prakash. Rahul gestured Rakhi suggesting that she should stop the conversation. A nurse handed a milk bottle to Rakhi who had the boy in her hand. When Rakhi began to feed milk to the baby, the nurse congratulated her for holding the child correctly. When the baby finished drinking the milk, Rakhi gently moved her fingers over the head of the boy and looked at his face and smiled as the baby opened his jet black eyes. Soon the contended sound emerged from the baby's mouth. Prakash stood next to Rakhi who said,

"See, he is happy. You were terrible at his age. You used to take a little milk from me and then used to make a moaning sound."

"Mum, please not now. You are exposing me to all present here. See they are laughing." Prakash was embarrassed. Rakhi put the baby near Seema. Soon, the baby was asleep.

All left the ward late in the evening. At home, everyone talked about the boy's weight, look and gentle smile. Suddenly, Lata cried loudly. Rakhi stood up and went near her and said,

"Please don't cry. This is the day of joyous celebration. Why are you crying?"

Lata, still crying uncontrollably, said in the broken voice,

"I failed to have a boy. I made my husband and daughters unhappy."

"Please don't say that. You know my good friend has six daughters and she never ever said about not having a boy. She is very proud of her children. Don't cry, be happy to have two lovely daughters and Seema has presented us both with a lovely boy. It is time to be joyous and celebrate the occasion." Sital brought water for her mum who took a sip and wiped her tears.

"Now please smile, you are going to be in a colour photo." Prakash was ready with a camera. Lata managed to show a smile as her face was painted with a white flash.

They visited Seema and the boy in the ward for two days. On home coming day, Prakash went alone to the hospital and helped Seema to gather clothes and other miscellaneous items. Before entering the house, Seema and the baby stood outside near the front door. Rakhi brought welcoming Thali (Plate) containing little rice grains, red Kankoo, a few flower petals, small lamp containing Ghee, and some milk. A little milk was added to water in a copper jug for cleaning the base frame of the door.

Seema followed the instructions, much against her wish, from Rakhi. Lata and Sital stood inside the house, behind Rakhi. Seema washed the base and the side frames of the door. Then, using the red Kankoo, she made straight vertical equidistance marks, three on each side, on the frames and sprinkled rice grains followed by laying of a single petal of rose on each mark. Rakhi then impressed a small red Kankoo mark on Seema's and the baby's forehead, followed by some rice attachment on the Kankoo. Finally, Rakhi took some water in her right hand and sprinkled over the mother and the baby. Then, she welcomed both with a kiss on cheeks. She hugged Prakash and gave him a kiss on his forehead as he entered the corridor.

They were escorted into the living room where a cot was placed near the fire place. The boy, well wrapped, was placed in the cot. Everyone came near the baby and made funny gestures frequently until the baby started to cry. They all scampered as Seema attended the baby. The house atmosphere turned into laughter and happiness. Soon the lunch was served.

Rakhi prepared two varieties of vegetable curries; one was of aubergines and potatoes and other of lady fingers with onions. Additionally, she made pilaf rice and lentils curry and sweet dish made of semolina with milk, sugar and nuts. She placed the plates and the cutlery on the dining table, adorned with new table cloth. Prakash lent his hands by bringing various food items. Lata stayed with Seema and Jivan admiring the baby. Sital sat quietly in a corner of the room. Rahul put small hand towels on chairs. All enjoyed the food and drinks and talked about the baby in the house.

It is a tradition that on the sixth day of the birth, Goddess Saraswati comes at night to write his future. For this, blank white papers, sprinkled with Kankoo, and a small pen made of wood for Saraswati to write on the paper, are put under the boy's bed overnight. The paper is then folded on the following day and kept in the house.

The boy was named Amar.

The relationship between Seema and Rakhi remained tense as Amar grew up. However, Rakhi had the full and free access to the baby. Soon, Rakhi and Rahul began to take him for a car ride after his lunch. Seema found a part time job in the local area. She worked from 8am till 2pm every day. Meanwhile, Rakhi gave devoted care of Amar and developed close relationship with the boy. Seema, having noticed the relationship, was quite happy generally but she kept dialogues to a minimum with Rakhi. If there was something that Seema didn't approve, she would make a protest and show how things should be done, e.g. putting a nappy on in a particular way. Rakhi felt insulted but didn't argue and simply followed the instructions. Here, there was a conflict of two different methods used for a newly born child. Rakhi had brought up Prakash and everything she did for her son was approved by the local nurse. Then, there is Seema who followed rigidly the instructions on the labels of various items. Rakhi did not argue with her as she loved Amar intensely and was willing to do whatever she wished.

At the age of 3, the first ceremony of cutting Amar's hairs was performed by a priest in the temple in Dudley. Kiran, Kamini, Vasant, Rakhi, Rahul, Prakash and Seema's parents and sister, Sital attended the ceremony. The local barber was invited for his service. It is said that this ceremony was conducted for a hygiene reason. In an agrarian society, the herbal medicine was primarily used to deal with health problems. There were doctors and hospitals but people didn't have money to pay for their services. Some well to do families who could afford the treatment, also resorted to the herbal treatment at first. The heat and dust, mal nutrition and poor hygiene condition in a village invited many health problems. If the head of a child was infected, it was shaved off to prevent accumulation of external pollution and facilitated easy cleaning and application of medicine. However, this system became a tradition as the time passed by and every newly born child has to go through the hair cut ceremony even today. Of course, many of the modern generation don't accept this tradition. Seema followed the family tradition.

Amar didn't make any fuss whatsoever. He appeared to be curious of what was happening to his head. Occasionally, he looked at Rakhi who talked to him.

"Hello my darling Amar, he (pointing at the barber) is taking your hairs off the head. Are you OK?"

Amar affirmed by shaking his head disturbing the barber. The onlookers laughed uttering, 'Oh you poor little boy'. Lata said her piece, Amar, what is the barber doing to your head?"

"Cutting hair" As Amar replied, he showed slight annoyance to his head being pressed downward to the maximum causing tension in his back. The barber immediately released his grip on Amar's head.

Amar, looking at Seema, said,

"Mumy, I don't want this."

Seema hurriedly went to him and held him to her chest and said,

"OK, my darling. There is only tiny hair left in the front. It has to be removed. I will hold you while it is removed, OK?"

Amar agreed and looked at Prakash.

"Dady, come here" he said.

Prakash moved towards him and sat next to him. The barber removed the bit of hair and Seema ran her fingers over Amar's head to remove loose hairs. Prakash lifted Amar and walked towards Rakhi; she held Amar and kissed his bald head. Amar smiled.

After the ceremony, as all began to disperse for the lunch at Kiran's house, Seema made sure to put a cap on Amar's head. It was Prakash's cap with initial NY. After the lunch, Rahul family drove back home.

The relations between Rakhi and Seema drifted more apart, to the point that Rakhi suffered more from physical and psychological problems. Once, when Rahul and Rakhi sat in the living room, in the early morning, Prakash joined them, his face looking grim.

"What is it, Prakash?" asked Rahul.

"Dad, I didn't have any sleep last night. She was complaining about the atmosphere in our house etc. She accused me of being coward as I haven't taken the charge of the house finances. She declared that she didn't like mum and wants to live separately from this house. What do I do now?" Prakash kept his head down as he put the question.

After a momentary look at Rakhi whose eyes began to fill with tears, Rahul said,

"Son, you have to decide. You have your family now. Please don't think that I am trying to avoid the issue. We are sad to hear about separation. Look, your mum has started crying. I am shocked. However, what should matter to you is that you take good care of them. You have our blessings. Let us know if you need anything. Where will you go? Have you found a place to live? I hope you don't go to live with your in-laws in Leeds."

"No dad, we will not go there under any circumstances. I don't know where we'll live." As Prakash was saying that, Seema came downstairs and stood near the door and asked Prakash,

"Well, are you coming? If you don't want to, it is fine by me. I can live separately somewhere without any problems. Don't think that I would run to my parents." She waited for the answer.

Rahul and Rakhi said nothing. Prakash got up and went upstairs. Seema followed him. Rakhi was crying uninterruptedly and began to say,

"Oh God, what have I done to deserve such punishment? I have never thought wrong of them. They have played a dirty trick on us just to take my son and Amar away from us. Why suddenly this separation? Where will they stay? It is a dull and wet weather. Why don't you find out where they are going to stay?" Rakhi told Rahul.

"Alright, my dear, you stop crying. We don't need any health problems. Please go upstairs and lie down in the bed. Did you take your asthma medicine today?"

"Yes." Rakhi stood up and made her way to the bedroom. Prakash came running down and enquired if Rahul had £100 cash he would need.

"Yes, I will give you the money. Do you have any idea where you will go from today?" Rahul asked.

"I have no idea, Dad. Seema doesn't say where we will be going." Prakash said in a soft voice.

"Why then she has decided to leave now? Surely, she ought to know where you will be going. Do you know something that I don't?" said Rahul.

"She is not talking to me now. Please give me the money now. I will let you know the details of the place later." said Prakash.

Both went upstairs and Rahul gave £100 to Prakash. Rakhi made no comment when Prakash took the money and went out of the room.

"Why did you give the money?" said Rakhi as she sat up in the bed.

"He gave me no reason. I suppose he needs cash for any emergency during the move. I asked him where they will go from here today and he said that Seema is not saying anything to him. I find it very strange, don't you?"

"I bet her parents must have planned all beforehand allowing Seema to raise this question of separation now. Otherwise, they can't leave this house today, can they?" Rakhi had a quick thought.

"You are right, my dear, yes, they know where they are going today. Why did Prakash lie to me?"

"I won't be surprised to know that he is forbidden to say anything now about the place" Rakhi concluded.

"Yes, perhaps you are right. If it is so, I think we shouldn't stop them to take whatever they want for their place. They will need utensils, bed sheets and pillows, groceries and spices etc. Let them have it. Do you agree?" Rahul asked.

"Sure, they can have anything from this house, including the dining table, cutlery and spoons and knives, anything really. Finally the conniving people have succeeded in separating Prakash from us, something that Lata wanted to do much earlier. Now that we are getting old and disable, they have struck to destroy us further. God will not let them have peace, you watch." Rakhi broke down and cried. Rahul was sadly disappointed too. He went down stairs and set quietly on the sofa.

In the next two days, Lata, Jivan and Sital helped to move things out of the house. The whole movement confirmed Rahul's suspicion of preconceived move. Now it was a question of getting the address of their new place. When they finally were about to move out of the house, Rakhi and Rahul stood near the front door and watched Seema and Amar entering the rear of her parents' car, Amar saw Rakhi and indicated that he wanted to go to MA (Rakhi). Lata held Amar and came near Rakhi. As the latter stretched her arms to take Amar, she began to cry. Amar looked serious and hugged Rakhi. The pain of separation was so severe that Rakhi nearly fainted. Rahul took Amar and kissed him saying goodbye as Lata whisked Amar away to her mother. Prakash stood in front of Rakhi and cried,

"Mum and Dad, forgive me for leaving you like this. But for Amar, I would have told them that they can take Seema away."

Rahul hugged Prakash and said,

"Son, don't worry about us. We will be OK. We hope that you have a happy life. Take care of Amar, he is very special. He is the progenitor of our family. Go my son. Be brave." Rahul walked away and wiped his tears before facing Rakhi. She kissed him and ran her fingers in his hair and held her face, saying,

"My dear son, don't worry about us. We will meet again. Go and take care of yourself and my dearest Amar. Bring him here whenever he wants to see MA." She turned around and went inside the house.

Both, Rahul and Rakhi sat in the front room silently for some times. Rakhi fell asleep on the sofa. After a while, the asthma attack started. Rahul ran upstairs to fetch the ventilator. It took a while for the attack to subside. They left the room and went upstairs to bed.

The house had to be sold as Rahul couldn't afford the expenditure to maintain it. Prakash and Seema moved locally in Langley, into a pre-war house with two bedrooms, small livimg room and kitchen. The wall decoration was typical of the fifties era; vertical red wide strips over faded dark yellow background wallpaper created a depressive atmosphere. The wooden windows with rotting frames were covered with stained yellow net curtains. There was a distinct smell of damp in the house. There were two sofa units, one double and one single. The dining table was positioned in a corner of the living room.

Prakash was contemplating the purchase of a house nearby where his parents were to live. Seema and her parents didn't like the idea but Prakash stuck to his plan so that he can serve his parents. A bungalow was chosen for Rahul and Rakhi in the local area. Part of the money that came from the proceeds of sale of the previous house was utilised in purchasing the bungalow. However, Seema demanded her share of the proceeds and Rahul had to borrow some money from the bank to complete the purchase of the bungalow.

Rakhi couldn't get over the whole incident. She spent many hours without uttering a word. Her eyes were full of water and her face looked sad. Rahul was concerned about her. He tried to cheer her up by taking her for a car ride over her favourite routes. They often visited the Windsor area; they spent an hour or so by the riverside. Still, she remained seriously depressed. He would buy her favourite ice cream or hot chips but this time she refused to have any of those.

It took some time for Rakhi to come to accept the reality of life. Rahul looked after her well. She had the things she desired so much for a long time. She bought gold jewellery and saris of her choice irrespective of the cost. Rahul and Rakhi attended few weddings in India and the USA. But, soon the time came to note her health problems. She constantly suffered from severe pain in the back due to the fractured coccyx. She got used to taking several painkillers. Whenever she was short of some tablets, she panicked. When her doctor noticed that she was helping herself to extra painkillers, Rahul was made strictly responsible for seeing the prescribed use of the drugs correctly. This created a friction between both and life became difficult to run. In the end, Rahul couldn't bear to see her suffering and constant pleading for more tablets. He made an exception some times and gave her minimum dose of extra tablets. She wouldn't accept a different company made painkillers even though the end result was the same. Rahul was more stressed than ever before. He began to lose his weight. The food became a problematic issue. Whereas Rahul would eat beans on toast, Rakhi wouldn't and waited for some vegetable curry and Roti or rice for her dinner. Rahul never lost his temper and lovingly served and cared for her. Friends and relatives helped by providing vegetarian meals. But, Rahul couldn't rely all the time on their generosity. Then, he began to prepare meals with the help from Rakhi. She sat on a chair and instructed Rahul on how to cook various foods. In time, Rahul became very expert in cooking variety of curries and rice etc.

One morning, she pulled out a letter from her purse and gave it to Rahul and said,

"After my death, hand over this letter to Lata."

Rahul read the letter and looked at the dejected face of Rakhi. He sat next to her and held her hand and said,

"Darling, under the circumstances we agreed that Prakash is to have a life of his own with Seema. We mustn't feel sad all the time. We have to keep our hands open and forge ahead by making our lives as good as we can make them. What will I achieve by giving this letter to Lata after you are gone? Why talk about you leaving this world? You will get depressed further. That will not be a good thing, will it?" Rahul looked at her watery eyes.

"I feel so sad, my dear, so sad." She burst into incessant crying. Rahul held her closer and whispered,

"I know my darling, I know. Shush now. Crying isn't going to help us both. Do you think I don't miss Prakash? Let's go downstairs and look at today's post."

Rahul picked up the post and both took places in the living room. One of the letters was a wedding invitation from Rakhi's relations living in Harrow. It was regarding a son's marriage. After reading the details, Rakhi's face brightened up. She said,

"We must attend this wedding. We will have to give a gift of a fairly expensive sari to my sister-in-law, Indu and a gift of gold to the boy. Poor thing, she will be feeling very sad as her husband, my cousin, will not be sharing the happy occasion."

"I know, he died some months ago from a heart attack." Rahul affirmed.

"As the wedding is in a fortnight, we don't have much time. Let's go shopping today, darling."

They went upstairs in the bedroom. She opened the cupboard for a sari. Rahul could see the fountain of happiness oozing out from her face. He realised that the gift items were going to be expensive. There was a shortage of money more so now than before. They made full payments for the mortgage, all the utility bills, and council tax. Despite a generous overdraft facility, they ran short of money at the end of each month. There was very little saving left. Rahul's facial expression reflected the concern; Rakhi noticed that and said,

"I know why you look so worried, my dear. It's the money, isn't it? Don't worry; I have some cash saved up. What's the present balance in the account?"

"Right now the account is fully overdrawn. However, do you remember the visit by Ghirther uncle and aunty from the USA? Before returning to India from here they gave me one hundred and one dollars, remember that?"

"Yes, you still have it?"

"They are in the secret section of my wallet". Rahul laughed. Then, he took out the wallet from his jacket and removed the money, and said,

"And look, I have twenty five pounds too. Let's change the dollars and find out how much money in total we will have."

Despite difficulty in walking without a stick, Rakhi got ready enthusiastically.

After exchanging the dollars, they went to their favourite sari shop in Wembley. A sari shop, mainly located in an area of dense Asian population, displayed a variety of cotton and silk saris, blouses and artificial jewellery. It also sold men's clothes—readymade suits, scarves and shirts. All the latest fashion saris were displayed in the front and side windows of a shop. The choice was wide and varied, from plain cotton to embroidered artificial and pure silk items.

A customer would notice a distinct fresh smell of new materials, taken out from large bales of goods, imported mainly from India and Japan. The shop had many bright lights which added sparkles to intricately woven embroidered red, yellow, green and blue saris and other items. The owner of the shop, where Rakhi shopped regularly, appreciated her honesty, charm and considerate opinions. She never hassled the staff. Other clients gave a lot of bother to the staff over the price of goods. The owner sympathised with Rakhi's health problems. She was a good customer. Her relationship grew further with the manager. On Diwali day, Rakhi insisted on having an expensive silk sari despite having limited money. The manager agreed to let Rakhi have the sari and pay after.

When the payment was made on the subsequent visit, the staff and the manager were impressed by the honesty and punctuality shown by both. Not all customers were punctual. Some never paid. From that day, Rakhi was declared openly, in the presence and witness of the staff, as sister of the manager. Every Diwali day, she was given the choice of selecting her favourite sari as a present from the manager. In return, she presented specially prepared sweets for the Diwali festival to him and the staff members.

Today, Rakhi took an hour to select a dark green embroidered silk sari and matching material for the blouse for Indu. Rahul stood in a corner and conversed with a staff member to pass the time. Rakhi looked at many saris. During that process, she came up to Rahul and said,

"Can I have a beautiful sari?"

He could see that she was quite determined to have the sari. She dragged him to the counter where her chosen sari was displayed.

"Have you found the present for Indu yet?" asked Rahul.

"Yes, this is the one and the other one is for me". She eagerly looked at Rahul. He felt the silky material of her choice of light green and white sari and said,

"Darling, this will be very expensive, you know that, don't you?"

She stepped back a bit and said,

"I never get what I want" She looked at him dispiritedly. Rahul knew that look well.

"How much is for this one?" He asked the manager waiting behind the counter.

"Sir, we are not asking for the money. So there is no question of price for the sari that my sister wants. She can have it as an early Diwali gift now."

Rakhi's face lit up with broad smile. Rahul was stunned by the gesture.

"So, I suppose the same goes for the other sari too" Rahul pushed his luck.

"No Sir, that one is expensive but I am going to reduce the price from £95 to £75. I am doing this because earlier my sister expressed her concern about lack of money."

"Really Rakhi, you shouldn't be talking about our personal finances" said Rahul.

"O.K., please wrap up these saris etc" instructed Rahul as he paid for the sari to be gifted. But then, Rakhi approached a lady member of staff and asked,

"Can I have the matching blouse for my sari ready within a week? How much will it cost to make?" she enquired.

Rahul heard £21, the cost of making the blouse. He asked the manager.

"Will you not make it free as it is a gift to your sister?" The 'brother' laughed and said,

"Sorry, the material for the blouse is free, the cost of making the blouse is £21, to be paid to a third party. I am sorry."

"Surely you can afford £21 for me?" said Rakhi without looking at Rahul. He looked at her momentarily in silence. The entire staffs were anticipating a reply.

"Of course my darling, I am all yours" Rahul bowed to her. Everyone laughed. Then, walking out of the shop, Rakhi was gently and quietly warned by Rahul.

"Now look my dear, don't say to me that you want this or that jewellery for yourself when we go into the jewellers' shops, O.K.?"

Rakhi was reminded of her usual habit.

"All right, all right. It's always like that for me, isn't it?" Rakhi was cross. Rahul ignored that. Upon entering in a brightly lit shop that had many counters displaying variety of gold items, Rakhi asked,

"What shall we get for the boy, a ring or a chain?"

"Whatever you fancy, perhaps, a gold ring would be less expensive than a gold chain." Rahul looked straight at Rakhi through the mirrored wall. She silently looked at both items presented by a sales lady. The latter gave an appraisal based on the weight, quantity of gold and the labour cost of making the items. Rakhi paid no attention to the sales lady's talk. She held the ring in her hand and asked Rahul for his opinion,

"Looks good; perhaps just the type the boys go for now-a-days."

"How much is this?" Rahul asked the sales lady.

"It's eleven grams, Sir. The price is £45 plus VAT, making a total price of £52.87."

"Isn't that too much, darling?" Rahul asked for Rakhi's view. Rakhi quietly murmured,

"It is O.K. but haggle for £48"

"Please make it £48 as we have £50 only with us today. We want to buy some vegetables also." Rahul requested.

"Sir, it can't be done. I have already given you a discounted price. However, let me ask my manager." She looked a bit annoyed as she went towards the office and came out immediately. The manager followed the lady to the place where Rahul and Rakhi were waiting.

"Hello, Ben (Sister), I believe you like this ring and want to have it for £48. It is a gift for a groom you are related to, is it?" The manager, smiling a little, asked Rakhi.

"Yes, for my late cousin brother's son" said Rakhi. The manager looked at Rakhi's serious face and deliberated. Then he said,

"O.K., this time you can have it for £48. But, please don't ask for a reduction next time. Other customers hear this and they will ask for me."

The manager went away. The ring was put in a nice velvety blue box and handed to Rahul.

"Let's go, Rakhi" said Rahul. She was looking at a gold set.

"You are not thinking . . . ." before Rahul could finish the question, Rakhi said,

"Don't worry my dear; I am not going to buy anything now"

Rahul noted the last word 'now' as it meant an anticipated future purchase. They walked out of the shop.

Two days before the wedding, Rakhi and Rahul went to attend the pre-wedding ceremony at the house in Harrow. Rakhi wore the new light green and white sari and the matching blouse. Also, from her jewellery box, she had picked the matching necklace, earrings and bangles that had light green and white zirconium stones. Rahul complimented,

"Wow, the beauty queen of my heart, you will be the show case girl today. The others will be jealous. In fact, am I not right to assume that you will be the only lady with such a fine sari and jewellery?"

"Wait and see, there will be other ladies with fine saris and jewellery too. Today is the first of three days' of wedding ceremonies. So, all the ladies will be well-dressed. Only you men will be wearing jeans and shirts. You people don't have the sense of occasion." Rakhi said as she was adjusting a pleating of her sari. She then sprayed her favourite Lily of the Valley eau de cologne all over her clothes.

"Do you have to bathe in that stuff? The heavy scent gives me a headache." He waved his arms to shift the fragrance.

"Oh, be quiet. You always say that. I like it this way". Rakhi said as she sat on the stool. She looked tired.

"Are you O.K.?"

"I am having pain in my right hip. It is a burning sensation. Let me rest a while; I will be alright soon." She was breathing heavily. She inhaled ventilator puffs four times as her asthmatic attack started. Rahul switched on the fan as she began to perspire. He was concerned,

"Shall we cancel the idea of going to Harrow?"

"No, no, I will be alright." She began to relax. Her breathing was becoming normal. She wiped her facial perspiration and told him to switch off the fan.

"What are you going to wear?"

"The pin striped suit and pink shirt with the matching tie, will that be OK?"

"That should be fine. It's just that I think you shouldn't wear jeans and t-shirts."

With the gifts wrapped and an envelope containing the customary eleven pounds as a gift for the groom, Rahul and Rakhi left home by car for Harrow. A customary payment as a gift varies in amounts depending on how close a relationship is with the bride/groom family. Half way to the place, Rahul asked if she was well. Rakhi looked at him and began to hum a song relevant to the GANESH ceremony. GANESH, the elephant God, dispels the darkness of ignorance and removes obstacles.

"Alright, we are happy then, good for you. That song you are humming reminds me of my mum. She was good at singing wedding songs. Hey, wouldn't it be great if she was with us today?" Rahul's voice became sentimentally frail.

"I know that Ba sang well. I learnt all the wedding songs from her but now after all these years, I have forgotten most of them. Yes, I would have been over the moon if she was here today. I wonder what God has done to her soul." Rakhi looked at the passing cemetery. She was thinking that God would give her soul an eternal peace and place. She believed in this. She was of the opinion that all her good thoughts and works for others will put her in a better place for reincarnation in future.

On their arrival, Rakhi went to join the ladies who were out in the backyard preparing various food items, such as savouries for a pre dinner snack and vegetable and yoghurt curries and rice for lunch. One of the favourite curries was made of aubergine and potatoes. Rakhi stood inside the kitchen, near the door leading to the women's work area outside. She was welcomed by two ladies who were frying Pakoras. The women were bathed in sweat due to the hot air created by the bright sun and the heat from the gas burners. The aroma of food spread all around and inside the house. The men did the heavy work, lifting things like oil drums and frying pans that were required for the preparation of various food items. They helped themselves to hot Pakoras and munched away as they worked.

There was a half an inch high step to cross before going to the outer work area from the kitchen. Rahul was engaged in framing the opening shot of the picture of Ganesh printed in vivid red, gold and yellow colours and seated on a red throne with his favourite LADOOS (round sweetmeat balls) in His left hand. Rahul was asked by Indu, the house lady to make a film record of the ceremony. He, being a keen amateur film maker, always carried his video camera. He often made films of weddings for the relatives.

Rakhi made an effort to cross the step with the aid of a walking stick. As she lifted her right foot to move forward, she lost her balance and her foot slipped. Two men rushed towards her to stop her falling on the concrete floor. Immediately, a person brought a chair for Rakhi. She screamed loudly. Her face quickly turned blood red and she began to cry like a baby saying in a broken voice,

"Please, call Rahul. I am feeling a burning sensation in my right hip. I cannot take the pain."

She was shaking as Rahul came running to the scene. As he was informed of the event, he held her gently by her shoulders and said,

"Oh my darling, what has happened to you?" She could not say a word. She began to shake. He wiped her tears.

"Has someone called for an ambulance?" Rahul looked at the people standing nearby.

"Yes, it will be here soon." said someone.

"I can't stand the burning pain in my hip, darling. I heard the cracking sound as I was about to fall." Rakhi couldn't stop crying.

"Will you please inform my son Prakash about this?" Rahul looked at Indu.

"Don't worry; I am to phone him now. I have the phone number." said Indu.

As soon as the ambulance arrived, the paramedics examined her pulse and blood pressure. They decided to take her to the nearest hospital. Rahul was informed that she could have a fractured hip. It was getting dark by the time Rakhi was admitted to the Accident and Emergency area. She was put on a bed in a cubicle. Rahul observed that there were a few nurses running around madly and three doctors in white overalls busy looking at x-rays and documents. The whole area was full of patients.

Soon a nurse came and checked Rakhi's temperature, pulse and blood pressure. Rakhi wanted to pass water. Rahul stopped one of the nurses and asked for a bedpan. She pointed towards a room full of items and said,

"Please pick up a pan from that room."

She hurriedly made her way towards another patient. Rahul picked up a pan and came near Rakhi and wondered how he was going to assist her. She, by now, was desperate. She couldn't manage to lift her bottom as the pain was severe. Rahul tried to assist her gently and finally the pan was placed in the right place. It was getting very hot. After an hour, Rakhi yelled,

"When will a doctor come to see me? I can't put up with this pain anymore."

Her face was full of agony and she was crying. Rahul went near her and stroked her forehead, saying,

"I am sorry my darling, but there aren't many nurses and doctors here. It is Friday and perhaps the most of the staff have gone home."

Rahul caught the attention of a nurse and asked if a doctor would come to see Rakhi soon. She said,

"Sir, I am very sorry for the delay. We are aware of your wife's situation and have called a specialist doctor to see her. He has been called back from his home. I will give a pain killing injection after I finish with the patient who is badly injured. Sorry."

Another half an hour had passed. Then, a young female house doctor, dressed in a white overall came to administer pain killing injection. A nurse was told to bring the x-ray machine. After the x-rays, the doctor informed Rahul that the specialist would soon examine her. She said,

"In my view, she has a fractured right hip and that is why she is in great pain. The morphine shot will soon alleviate some pain. I am sorry for the delay in seeing her. On Fridays, we get quite a lot of emergency patients."

The specialist in plain clothes accompanied by the lady doctor approached Rakhi's bed and asked,

"How long has she been here? She looks in great pain." He began to examine her.

"She was brought here about two hours ago. The x-rays are here for your examination, Sir." Both doctors headed towards the x-rays.

The consultant came near the bed and informed Rahul,

"She has a broken hip and in the morning, she will have to be operated on. I suggest you go with her to the ward where she will be till morning. You go home as soon as you can. The ward sister will inform you about the time when she will come out of the theatre; you can visit her then." The consultant left the cubicle.

Rahul went near the anxious Rakhi who seemed a bit relaxed. He informed her about everything the consultant said.

"Oh my God, why has this happened to me? The x-rays taken a few weeks ago had shown that everything was ok. How come now I have a fractured hip?"

Rakhi was frightened of the prospect of having to undergo an operation for the replacement of the hip. She was of the opinion that she wouldn't be able to walk normally after the operation.

"I suspect that when you put your body weight on the right hip as you tried to come out of the kitchen door, the hip joint couldn't take the pressure and split. We know that your bones are fragile and liable to break due to osteoporosis. I think this is what happened. I understand you being worried about the loss of normal walking ability, but consider how lucky you are to have the replacement tomorrow. Many people have to wait for a long time for their hip operations". Said Rahul.

She began to cry.

"Now don't cry my love please. Everything will be fine. The sister will inform me after the operation and I will come to the ward immediately. You will be well sedated and possibly won't come out of it for a long time. After the hip replacement, you will be able to walk and get rid of the pain. In this day and age, such operations are very successful. We don't have to worry, my dear" He stroked her forehead. A nurse gave a pain killing injection and informed Rahul that he should leave the ward as soon as she felt sleepy.

As Rahul drove towards the house, he felt very sad about the whole incident. It dawned on him that their life was about to undergo great changes. He realised the significance of the oncoming responsibility of looking after Rakhi and all the general domestic work. Before going to bed, Rahul informed Prakash on his mobile about the incident as Prakash didn't come to the A and E. Prakash said,

"I am sorry dad that I couldn't come to the hospital as I had to attend the board meeting which was to deal with my project. I am very sad to hear about mum. I give you my new address and telephone number now."

Rahul was relieved to note that Prakash wasn't residing far from the house. Prakash said that he would meet Rahul at the hospital on the following day.

Next day at noon, Rahul was informed of the successful outcome of the operation and that he could visit Rakhi in an hour's time. Rakhi was expected to come out of the sedation by then. Rakhi was still feeling sleepy when Rahul and Prakash came to see her. She managed to open her eyes to see them. Both were informed by the ward sister that the consultant had found complications during the operation. Contrary to his expectation of simply inserting a plate, he had to scrap a lot of soft bone area to replace the full artificial hip. Rakhi would remain in the hospital for twelve days.

"I see that she is being given blood. Why?" Rahul asked.

"She lost some blood during the operation. Don't worry, it is normal. She is fine and soon will come out of the sleep. Please don't give her anything to eat." After reassuring Rahul, she went away.

"Dad, what is happening to mum? It's one thing after another, isn't it? I hope that poor mum won't give up her willpower."

Rahul just looked at Prakash without saying a word. He knew that Rakhi was stressed due to Prakash leaving the house. It must have affected her daily. Though she used the walking stick, she shook as she moved about. Prakash stood up and went near Rakhi and put his hand over her forehead. It was hot, He reported his observation to a nurse.

"It is normal after an operation to have high temperature. I will be monitoring her temperature frequently."

"Dad, let me ask you this, not all patients have been given blood. Look around, none of them have a blood bag. Surely, some of them must have been operated on this morning. Do you see what I mean?" Prakash expressed his concern. Having scanned the ward, Rahul said,

"We don't know about this but I think you may be right. I am concerned about HIV and things like that. We hear a lot about the deaths due to wrong or infected blood. It is worth querying, but wait for a while until the nurse come to take her temperature."

Presently Rakhi woke up and said,

"Hi".

Her voice was croaky. Rahul got up and went near her and kissed on her forehead.

"We are sad to see you in this condition. The sister told us everything about the operation. How are you feeling now, my dear?"

"Fine, I feel very sleepy, thirsty and hungry. Have you brought any food?"

"Yes, but we are told that you aren't allowed food and drink. I am sorry darling." Rahul gently caressed her hand.

"My throat is dry." She yawned as she spoke and appeared to fall asleep. A nurse came to check her out.

"She said she was feeling very thirsty. When can she have a drink?" Prakash asked.

"She will feel that way due to the anaesthetic. By late this evening, she will be allowed a little water. You do know that she is not allowed to eat. She will be given tea and biscuits in the morning. Don't worry, she will be OK. Now, if you both will leave, please. I am to examine her dressing. You will be informed when to come to see her." She began to close the side curtains as Rahul and Prakash left the ward. They went to the hospital restaurant and had something to eat and drink.

Prakash noted his father's sad face and said,

"Come on dad, she will be all right. I know that she will not be able to walk normally, but at least will be able to walk without pain. Don't think that I am not concerned about her being in the hospital. Seema said that I shouldn't bother about mum as you were dealing with her. I felt sick hearing that and told her that I was to visit mum every day. I added that she needn't bother to visit mum. This morning, my father-in-law phoned to say that they would be coming to visit mum. I informed them that no one except us two were allowed to visit her. It was a lie, but they make me sick." His face was full of anger. Rahul simply looked at Prakash and said nothing.

After twelve days, Rakhi came home. Her progress was monitored by a district nurse and the family doctor. After a few weeks, she began to walk about little by little. She was eagerly looking forward to visiting the neighbours who were very pleased to see her. Also, she wanted to visit relatives but Rahul didn't approve of such activities so early. Rahul's feelings for her had intensified seeing her poor health. He vowed to help her in any manner from then onward. After six months, Rakhi was feeling confident about walking further distances. Rahul drove her to their favourite riversides, in Twickenham and Windsor. He could see greater happiness on her face. At the same time, he saw her making an extra effort to walk with signs of stress and pain.

"Darling, I am aware that my health imposes extra responsibility on you. I am sorry. I don't understand why I am going through this terrible problem in my life. Do you remember at one time we asked the GP to check my bones? She said that there was nothing wrong with my bones. Only one week ago before the recent incident, the x-rays had shown a hair line fracture of the right thigh. Why was it ignored? Look at me now, how I am suffering." Rakhi stared at Rahul.

"Well that is what the NHS has come to. Never mind darling, I know that from now onwards you would be feeling happy. Just take it easy. Remember, I am with you all the time. Just let me take good care of you. I can cook, clean things and take care of most of the things. I hope you enjoy life." Rahul kissed her.

"Come on, let's go home. It is breezy here in Windsor" Rakhi was helped to get off the bench. She slowly made her way to the car.

Many visitors came to see her; they brought flowers and gifts and specially prepared sweetmeats like Jallebi (Curly, like Catherine wheel, orange coloured sweet), Russomalay (split milk circular portions soaked in milk with pistachios, saffron and sugar) and spicy snacks. Rakhi enjoyed the company of visitors.

A year later, another disaster struck. She began to complain about pain in her left hip. One morning, at 4 am, she complained of burning pain in her stomach and left hip. A night doctor came to the house at 5:30 am and administered a pain relieving injection. With the doctor's presence the bedroom was filled with the smell of alcohol. After his quick departure, Rakhi felt no better. She began to cry loudly complaining of burning in her stomach. She then said that she wanted to pass water. Rahul was in a predicament, there was nothing like a bed pan in the house. He ran hurriedly to the kitchen and took a small stainless steel bowl and returned to the bedroom. Rakhi's face was full of agony. She apologised for the inconvenience.

"That is alright my darling. I have to lift your bottom to insert the bowl underneath?"

"Yeh."

As Rahul tried gently to raise her bottom, she yelled saying,

"I am so sorry but I cannot control the urine." With that, she passed urine on the bed. Immediately Rahul tried once more to insert the bowl underneath her bottom and succeeded. Just as well that happened as Rakhi now couldn't control the bowel movements. Rahul just managed to catch the output. After this frantic event, Rahul helped to move her gently on to the other side of the bed so that he could clean the spoilt bed sheet and clean the surface of the mattress. Rakhi kept shouting about pain. Rahul realised the seriousness of the situation. He expedited the cleaning and called an ambulance at 7 am. The ambulance arrived at 7:10 am.

After examination, the crew decided to take her to the local hospital's A and E section. As they arrived at the hospital, Rahul was advised to report at the reception desk in the general room. Rakhi's x-rays and blood samples were taken. The x-rays showed a fractured left hip. Another set of pictures were taken to confirm the fact. At 14:45, she was admitted to ward one where further blood samples were taken and a routine examination done. Then they waited for the consultant; he was otherwise engaged. He saw her on the following day. He was an elderly person wearing striped shirt and dark grey trousers. The decision to operate was made and at around 4 pm, she was taken to the theatre. At 7 pm, Rahul phoned to speak to her. She hadn't come out completely from the anaesthetic.

The doctors were concerned about her white cell counts; they diagnosed pneumonia. Antibiotics were given to her. She didn't feel like eating. But had fresh fruit juice and drank a lot of water. They were still concerned about her lungs also because of asthma. Her stomach was upset. A house doctor examined her and gave her some medicine to tackle the problems. However, she was not feeling well as her stomach remained upset.

Her condition began to improve slowly. She was weak still and had back pain. She began to take a little food. Rahul observed that the ward was primarily for very sick elderly disabled ladies. He wondered why Rakhi was admitted to such a depressing ward. There were conflicting instructions from various staff members. Rakhi was required to sit up for long hours due to a lung infection she had caught in the previous ward. Such pre-requisite necessity created extremely uncomfortable situation for her. She looked very tired. She had four spoonfuls of a rice based meal; two large cherries; and one pear. She complained of stomach pain, each time she had something to eat. But at no time was her stomach examined.

As she was expected to sit in a chair more often, she had severe pain in the calf of her left leg. A nurse agreed that if the pain increased in that position then she must lie flat on the bed. Pain had gone considerably after laying flat. They assumed that the burning sensation in the stomach was due to the chest infection. She felt better. Her food intake improved and she drank few glasses of glucose mixed water. She felt less tired. She could walk some 40 feet with ease with the frame.

Staffs were reluctant to respond to any requirements by the patients. Rakhi made several requests to lie down. She was firmly reminded that she must sit as she had a chest infection. Rahul observed that the nurses told patients what was to be done and had paid little attention to the patients' requirement. Whenever a patient asked for something, the staff continued to read a news paper or carried on their conversation. When patients required pan or commode the items were not presented quickly. The nurses would tell off the patients if their bed sheets were soiled. Thus, haste and insistence were the order of the day.

After the removal of stitches, Rakhi was permitted to go home. She was advised to continue with the exercises and medication.

Then, one morning at 5:30 am, Rakhi complained of burning pain in her stomach. Rahul tried to get the night doctor but no contact was possible for one and half hours due to technical problems. He called an ambulance at 8:15 am as she had vomited twice. On arrival, the ambulance crew, after routine examination of Rakhi, took her and Rahul to the local hospital. She was given an injection to relieve pain. At 9:25 am, a sodium chloride drip was attached. X-rays of her stomach and chest were taken. In the x-ray section, there was only one lady dealing with five patients. The x-ray showed that the stomach was o.k. but the doctor on duty decided to check Rakhi's pancreas. Another set of x-rays were taken. Blood tests were done once more. Pain killer tablets were given at 12:15 pm before the surgeon's opinion was sought. She was taken to a medium sized room, painted light blue, in ward 8 for a further examination.

The house doctor examined Rakhi who looked as if she was lost. A nurse brought an oscilloscope and attached the wires to Rakhi's various body parts. She was given another morphine injection. After applying a saline solution, Rakhi appeared to calm down for a while.

"Darling, give me some water please. My lips are very dry. What is happening to me?"

Her eyes were rotating more than before as if looking for something. Rahul got permission from the doctor to wet the Lollypop, a cotton ball on a small stick, and apply to her lips. As he gently rubbed the wet ball on her lips, she exclaimed,

"Ahh, that is nice, thank you my darling. Can I have one more time?"

On second application, Rahul said,

"My love, please don't ask me for more. The doctor told me to limit the application."

"But I feel very thirsty and dry. Please, give me once more, please."

She begged.

Prakash entered the room and stood besides Rahul. The latter sadly looked at him and said,

"It doesn't look good at all." He nearly burst into tears. Prakash held him and whispered,

"Please dad, don't cry. She will pull through. Don't give up and don't show your sad face to her. Let me talk to her."

Prakash held her hand and said,

"Hello mum, how are you feeling?"

She slowly looked at him and said,

"Oh my son, what is happening to me?"

"Everything is going to be fine, you will see."

"Dear, give me water, please"

Rahul pointed at the cotton ball. As Prakash applied the wet ball to her lips, she expressed a gentle smile and rolled her tongue over lips.

"Give me some more"

Prakash obliged. Soon Rahul took over the stick and inserted in a cup full of water.

"The doctor told me not to give more than two applications at a time."

Rahul informed Prakash. Two ladies in blue uniforms turned up to measure the pulse in Rakhi's legs. Rahul and Prakash stood silently for a while.

"I feel nothing" said one of the ladies whose face looked very serious.

"Yes, same here. She is turning blue" said the other.

"Please, can you tell us what is happening?" asked Rahul.

"There is no pulse in her both legs. We will send a nurse to remove fluid from her stomach." The ladies left. Soon, a nurse came with a long transparent plastic tube and began to insert it through Rakhi's nose.

"What is she doing? It hurts." Rakhi complained.

"It is for the removal of fluid in your stomach. You will feel better, mum." said Prakash as he looked at his father. They both realised that her condition was getting more serious. They silently witnessed the procedure involving insertion of one end of the tube in her nose and attachment of the other end to a large plastic bag. A dark green liquid began to flow into the bag. As the nurse left the room, Rahul went around her right side of the bed and held her left hand and gently caressed it.

"Why are you rubbing your hand?" She asked Rahul.

"Darling, I am rubbing your hand, not mine."

"You are going away" She cried out.

Rahul immediately put his hand on her forehead and said,

"My love, I am not going anywhere. I am here with you."

"Yes mum, we are here with you." said Prakash.

She turned her face to and fro and looked at both simultaneously.

Her face reflected fear and uneasiness. The nurse administered morphine injection.

"Please don't leave me." She said to Rahul as she tried to hold his arm. But, she couldn't move her arm.

"Why are you moving away?" Again she asked Rahul

"I am here, my darling. We are both here." Rahul quickly moved in a corner and began to cry. Prakash turned to him and said,

"I think I should find out from the doctor more about her." He left the room. Rahul wiped his tears and went near Rakhi who now was finding breathing difficult. She complained,

"Everything is burning inside, ohh, please help; do something. Give me some water."

She begged for help. Rahul took the wet cotton ball and applied over her lips. Suddenly, she held his hand and began to apply the ball to her lips. But, her hand lost the grip and fell on her chest. She began to breathe heavily. The doctor and Prakash entered the room. After seeing her breathing fast, the doctor went out quickly. Soon he entered the room again and informed Rahul that her condition was getting critical. He tried to shift her to the intensive care unit but there was no vacant bed available.

For the next three hours, Rakhi kept breathing unevenly fast. Once more, the doctor entered the room to see how Rakhi was breathing.

"What happens now, doctor? A patient could die under these circumstances. Is there nothing else that can be done?" asked Prakash as he looked at the closed eyes and heavy breathing of his mother. As the doctor said nothing, Rahul with tears in his eyes, asked,

"She doesn't deserve this. All her life she struggled to survive. Now she is struggling here again." Rahul slid down against the wall and sat down on the floor holding his head in his hands.

At 23.00 hours, the doors flung opened and two men entered the room with a bed trolley. Soon they moved Rakhi on the trolley and put an oxygen mask on her face. They rushed out of the room and along several corridors. Rahul and Prakash literally ran beside the trolley. Suddenly, she spoke,

"Where are you taking me? What is happening to me? It is burning fire inside."

She closed her eyes for the last time.

The rain of tears was flowing down Rahul's face as he tried to keep up with her. Two large doors flung opened and the trolley went inside the ITU. A nurse standing inside held open one door and said,

"Please wait here in this room. We will call you as soon as she is transferred to another bed". The door was shut.

Rahul was still crying. Prakash escorted him towards a dimly lit room and made him sit on a sofa. He sat next to him. He put his left arm over father's shoulder and consoled,

"Dad, please don't cry. She has a good chance to pull through this. She is now in the best hands."

"You know she isn't going to pull through. Oh God, I don't think we are going to hear her voice anymore." Rahul began to cry intermittently. It was a devastating realisation for him that both were about to lose a wonderful, kind and charming lady who had given the family her entire life. Her medical condition was not comprehended soon enough to make her live longer more in this world.

An elderly lady who saw Rakhi being taken in, looked at Rahul and softly whispered,

"God works in a mysterious way, Sir. Please don't cry. She will be alright. Look on the bright side. My husband has been inside for the last three days and he is still breathing. They told me that he wasn't going to make it. But, I am hopeful. So, please don't cry."

"Thank you for your kind words" said Prakash.

An hour later, they were allowed to go inside the ITU room. They silently stood near Rakhi and observed her deep breathing. She was wired up for her heartbeats and had several tubes inserted in her nose and mouth. She was covered up to her chin. She appeared to be relaxed, her eyes closed and the machine kept her alive. Rahul bent close to her face and softly spoke,

"Hello darling, I am here with you. I love you so much and I will be here with you. Don't worry." He was unable to think of something more to say. More tears began to flow down his cheeks. She squeezed her face tightly as if she was trying to talk back. But, due to the wires and tubes, she couldn't say a thing. The consultant advised Rahul and Prakash not to speak to her. Her eye brows flicked upwards. Rahul couldn't see her anymore and walked away after kissing on her forehead. Prakash followed Rahul to the outside room.

Later, the consultant called Rahul and Prakash in his office. He said,

"The stabilisation of her body was a prerequisite thing to prepare her for CT scan we are hoping to carry out so that the pancreas can be investigated by operation. We suspect pancreas malfunction. However, we aren't sure of the cause of the numbness in her legs and arms. The body is rejecting all the latest medication."

The consultant paused very briefly and looked straight into Rahul's eyes as he continued to say,

"Her blood pressure is dropping and there is only a five percent chance of her survival."

The consultant paused momentarily again and then walked near Rahul and put his hand on his shoulder as he said,

"We are doing our best. There is a very thin line between life and death. Even with the use of the best available medicine, her body keeps slipping towards death. I am sorry."

He walked away towards the doors.

Rahul went out of the room hurriedly and headed towards Rakhi's bed. He was shaking as he approached her. He looked down on her face which soon began to fill with his tears. Her face appeared soft and peaceful to him. He whispered to her,

"Go my Angel into the lap of our Father. He will take better care of you now. Please forgive me if I have hurt you and not fulfilled your wish."

Rahul broke down as he back stepped from her bed and turned his face away to a nurse standing by near him. He hugged her like a crying baby and said,

"I have lost my soul, Oh my God, how will I live alone now?"

Prakash stood near the doctor in charge. Rahul slid down crying on the floor. Prakash came near him and gently lifted him and hugged him. Prakash's eyes were full of tears. They slowly made their way towards the exit door. The doctor followed them outside the ITU room. He told Prakash to return to the unit before 10 am.

Rahul and Prakash left the hospital in the early hours of the morning. Rahul didn't wish to witness her death. Earlier in the day, Prakash and Seema went to the hospital to stay besides Rakhi. Prakash felt that he should be there to see his mum taking her last breath. He insisted that Seema should accompany him. Rakhi left this world at 10:25 am.

Prakash put TULSI (Fresh leaf of a sacred plant) and GANGAJAL (Water from the river Ganges) in her mouth. The consultant asked Prakash for Rahul's permission to conduct an autopsy to find out the cause of the other problems. Rahul granted his consent over Prakash's phone. Her funeral was arranged to take place in a week. The autopsy report stated that due to pancreatic and lung conditions, other organs had rapidly deteriorated. Blood poisoning had occurred.

Rahul's sister, Reena arrived from the USA. She undertook the responsibility for making all the relevant arrangements prior to the funeral. Apart from Rahul, Reena was the only other surviving member of Govind family. It was customary for her to undertake the total responsibility of arranging the ceremonial matters for the funeral. She specified who was to attend the pre-funeral bathing and dressing of Rakhi; ensured that items such as coconuts, red powder (KANKU), TULSI, Betel leaves and nuts, a garland made of fresh flowers, a lamp and thin garland made of sandalwood were available. She also made seating arrangements in the house for the people coming to pay their respects. Since no one in the family was in a position to cook food, a relative prepared and supplied food for all in Rahul's family.

PRE FUNERAL OF RAKHI

The lounge was filled to the brim with all the female friends and relatives. The men stood in the corridor and in the front area of the bungalow. Rahul sat on a sofa and his sister, Reena sat near him on the floor of the lounge. She looked at Seema and said,

"Seema, you will join us to attend the funeral director's place to wash and dress Rakhi before going to the crematorium".

Seema, who sat on a chair, swinging one leg and playing with her curls, wore a black sari with matching blouse. She didn't wear any jewellery. She glanced at the ladies fleetingly. The ladies were anxious to hear her confirmation. She said,

"I don't want to go there to see her. After all, she insulted me on many occasions. I don't care about her. You lot can go and do whatever is to be done".

The audience was shocked to hear her views. After a moment's silence, a gentle whisper between two women could be heard,

"What a nerve! Can you believe Rakhi could hurt a fly? What a cheek to say openly what she said?"

Reena looked at Rahul as he spoke to Seema,

"OK Seema, you don't have to go. Is that alright Reena?"

After deliberation, Reena looked towards Seema and said,

"That's fine, Seema, you don't have to come".

Seema's face turned very red. She got up quickly and hurriedly made her way into the kitchen where her parents were present. Jivan sadly spoke in a quiet voice,

"Seema, you shouldn't have said that in such an irate manner. This isn't the time to seek revenge in the presence of the ladies. This is all wrong."

"OK, she made a mistake. Now leave her alone." Lata defended Seema.

"Dad, I don't care about what they think. I never liked her; I told you both many times that if you want to keep relations with this lot then it's up to you. I won't have anything to do with this family"

After saying this, Seema stood in a corner. Her face reflected her anger. There was a pin-drop silence in the house. Then, an elderly lady in tears, who came from Rahul's village, looked at Rahul and said,

"My dear, look how the world has changed. Nowadays, the young people follow only their self interest. There is no value put on the established social rules. Don't feel too bad if she doesn't want to see Rakhi."

Rahul, wiping his tears, looked at the woman and said,

"Aunty, it's not her fault. If only I knew what the insulting remarks were. I would have sorted the problem long ago. I don't suppose we will ever know exactly what happened. Seema refused on many occasion to tell us what the insulting words were."

"But how could Rakhi insult anybody in this world? It was against her nature. She was very kind and gentle to everyone. She gave away her personal belongings to others without any hesitation. How could she have insulted Seema?" The voice of an angry woman came from the crowd.

"It is all over now. Be quiet." said the woman who sat next to her.

Reena organised the time and ladies to go for the dressing of Rakhi's body. Traditionally, the washing and dressing of the body is done by the members of the family and of the in-laws.

They drove to the place where Rakhi's body was kept. There was an eerie silence as they entered the sitting room. Photos showing Indian religious features were hung on one wall. A young lady directed Rahul, Reena and Rakhi's brother, KIRAN and sister-in-law, Kamini and their daughters to the room where the body was to be brought after the dressing. Reena, Kamini and her elder daughter went to dress Rakhi, kept in a separate wash room. After an hour, the ladies came out with an assistant pushing the trolley on which Rakhi was laid.

As soon as the trolley halted, KIRAN burst into tears. He went near her body and began to say loudly,

"I am terribly sorry, my dear sister, that I couldn't see you lately. Oh God, please forgive me".

He continued crying. Rahul approached him and put his arm on his shoulder, and said,

"What is the use of crying now? You were attending your sister-in-law who was on the verge of dying also. It is understandable why you couldn't visit Rakhi. It's all over now. Please stop crying and join us in the prayer."

All sat on the floor near the trolley and prayed for a while. They stood up and looked at Rakhi's body.

Rakhi looked stunningly beautiful, as if she was a bride about to get married. Her dress consisted of a blouse, a petticoat and a sari, all with exquisite embroideries and of a gorgeous pink colour. Her head was covered with the end of the sari. Her legs were covered with the matching coloured stockings and feet with pink slippers. As per tradition, her clothing, bangles and jewelleries were provided by Kiran. Her arms were adorned with her favourite coloured bangles. Her hands were clasped in the traditional 'Namaste' ('I bow to the God in you') after the wash. Rahul began to choke as he endeavoured to continue with the prayer.

A moment later, he went near Rakhi's face. He stroked her forehead and began to say,

"Aren't you going to ask me one more time for a drop of water, my darling? Please open your eyes. It's not enough to show your usual magnificent smile, dear"

His words broke up as he couldn't stop crying loudly. Kamini and Kiran held him on either side as he tried to hold Rakhi's arms. Suddenly, Rakhi's arms flung open and dropped on the either side of her body. Rahul was startled. He assumed that she didn't wish for that last drop of water after all. Reena fastened Rakhi's hands and put them on her stomach. The fingers were interlocked, indicating the final 'Namaste' to all present.

An hour later, they left the place.

One Early Morning, the Prayer

Fourteen days after Rakhi's funeral, having taken a morning shower, RAHUL put on clean clothes. He went into the dining room. The square shaped Mandeer, a little temple with half circular dome on top, had two glass plates on both sides and two doors in the front. The temple was fixed on the wall facing the easterly direction. Several small yellow and silver metal statues representing various images of Hindu Gods (Like Krishna, Rama, Shiva, Amba, Parvati, Ganesh and Hanuman) were kept inside the temple. One large Conch was kept in front of the statue of Lord Krishna.

Rahul cleaned and dried all the items with fresh water and applied the red Kanku on the foreheads of each statue. As he did that, he pronounced the name associated with each one, e.g.' OM, I bow to Lord Shiva', 'OM, I bow to Lord Krishna' and so forth. He placed small quantity of milk and fruit like banana or apple in front of Lord Shiva. Then, he lit a large joss-stick and turned it round several times in front of each statue saying the name of each image of GOD. Then, he lit a lamp and began to pray by moving it in a circular motion, once clockwise and then once anti clockwise. Finally, he passed his hand over the flame, pointing towards each statue, to offer the warmth of the light. After that, he rang a small bell requesting All Mighty power to hold peace everywhere in the universe, sky, water, earth, vegetation, and trees in the world. Rahul prayed ever since Rakhi was unable to pray due to her ill health. When he was a student in India, he believed in the Hindu concept of various images representing the Supreme Power.

Suddenly, he felt as if Rakhi had joined him. He actually glanced fleetingly on his right side and thought her translucent body was standing next to him. He quickly turned towards the Mandeer as he felt pain in his heart. His eyes began to fill with tears. As he started to wipe his tears, he dumped himself on the chair nearby.

Once more, he looked to find Rakhi. His body trembling, he began to cry loudly. He slowly rose to face the Mandeer. He looked at the several statues and in stuttering voice he asked,

"Oh Supreme Energy, my God, what did you gain by taking her away from me?"

Presently, the sunrays filtering through the side window fell on his face. With tears still flowing, he slowly turned his eyes to look at the sun. It was the same wavering diffused light he had seen in the park before. The mirage of the surging Chariot of Light reminded him of the voice he had heard in the local park.

'Why are you so depressed? Rise and carry on with the task of living. She has not gone away. She is around you all the time. Learn to look at her. She gave you all the happiness of a good life. Now, you fulfill her dream of you achieving happiness in your life.'

Rahul felt the same vibration as before. As he opened wide the window, he was engulfed by the bright light. He stopped crying. The early morning fresh air, full of rose fragrance, hit him to say,

'Go and live happily with the memories of good things she gave you'.